AF411607

Pure Senses

A MEDITATIVE JOURNEY IN SOUND AND VISION

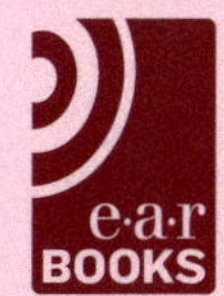

Our senses are the key to our understanding the world – right from the beginning; we have a nose to smell with, a pair of eyes to see, two ears to hear with. A mouth to taste with, two hands to touch. Nature has equipped human beings with a perfect system in order to enjoy life's enticements and sensual pleasures in all their variety. Let's take time to concentrate on our basic abilities of sensual recognition; they are a source of power, they give us strength and energy in order to face everyday challenges in a relaxed mood. Allow yourself to be lured into a sound and image world inviting you to open up your senses. Let your body and spirit unite…

PURITY MEANS COMMITMENT TO
THE ESSENTIALS.

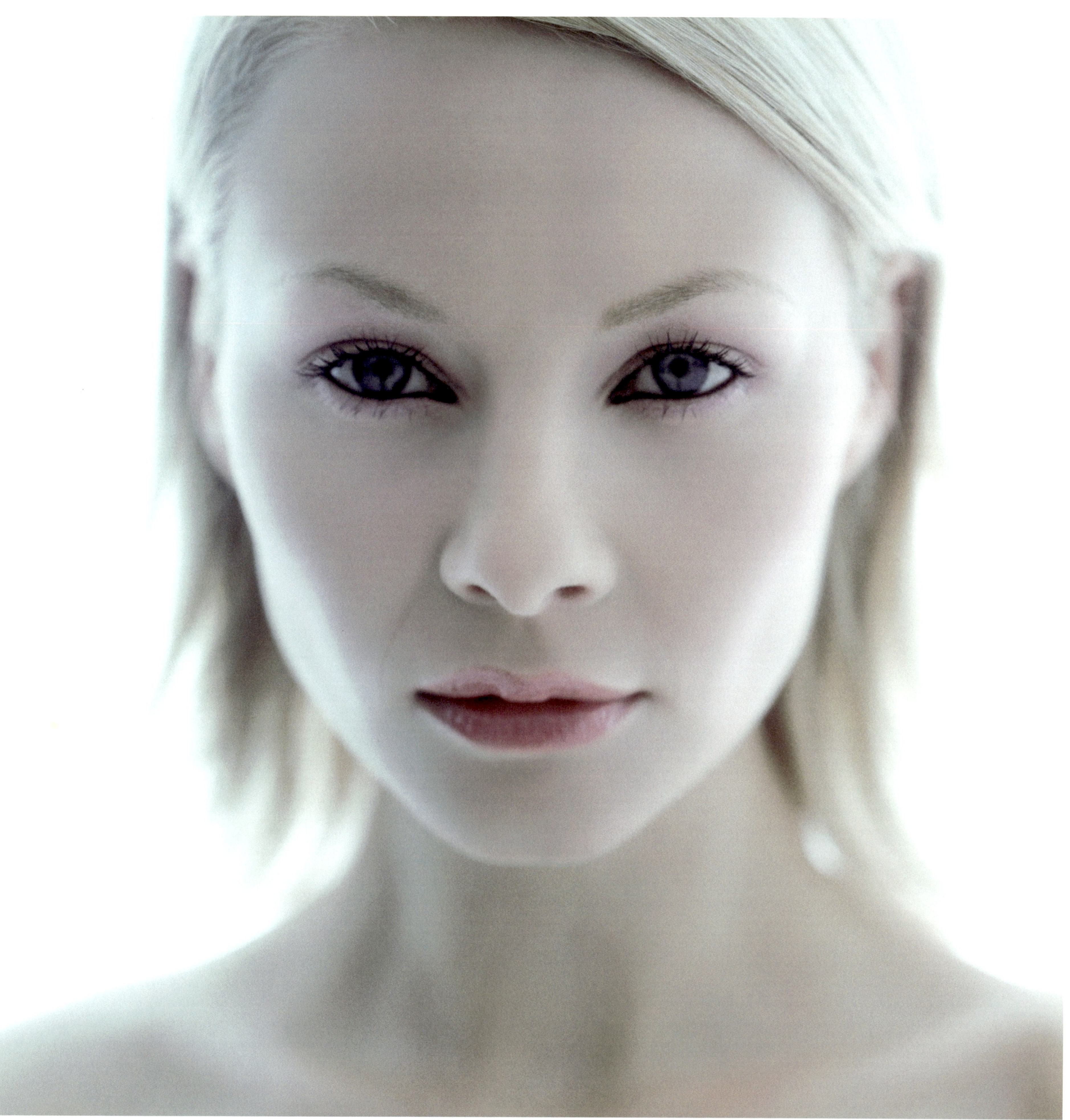

EVEN WITHIN YOUR OWN FOUR WALLS YOU
CAN BROADEN YOUR HORIZONS.

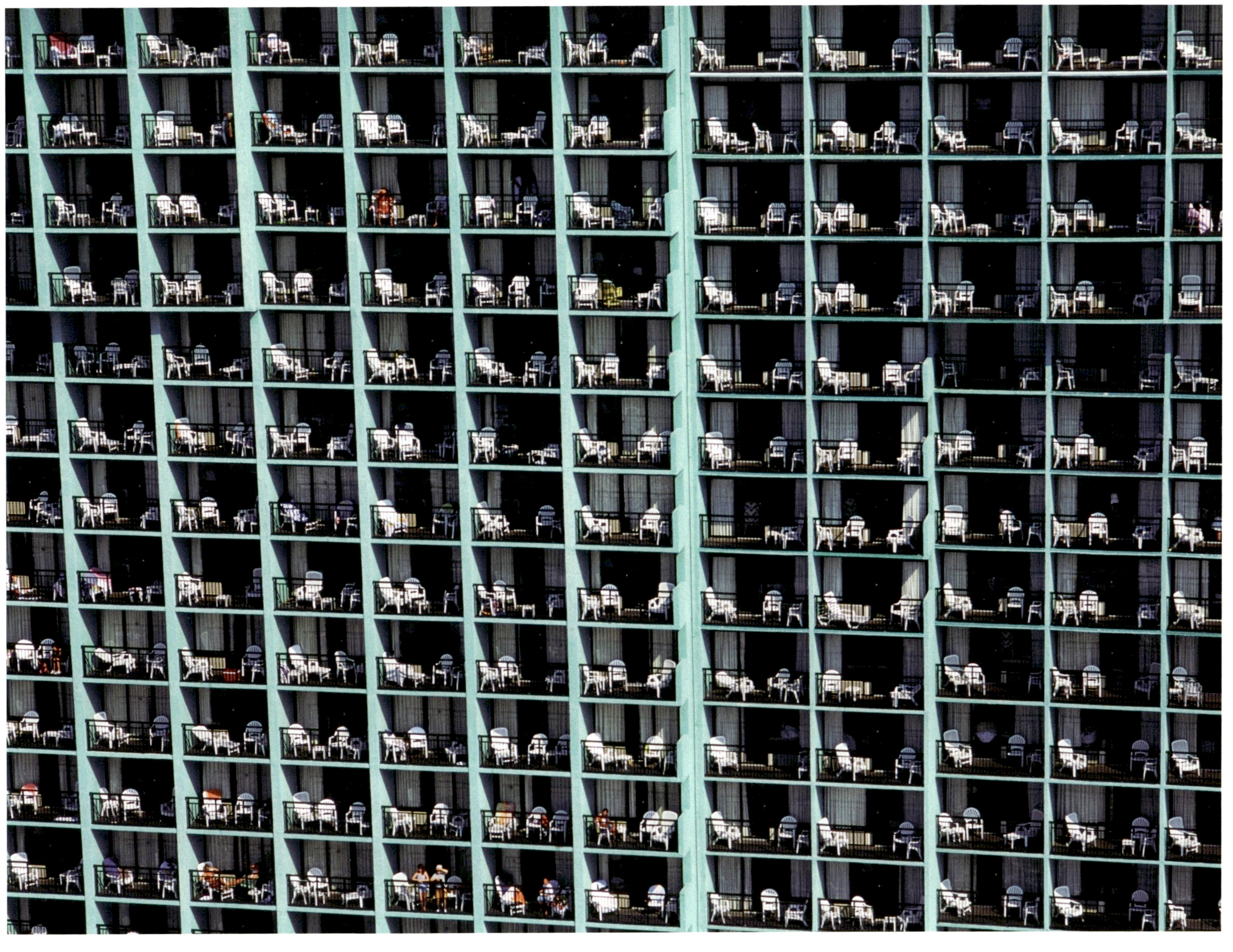

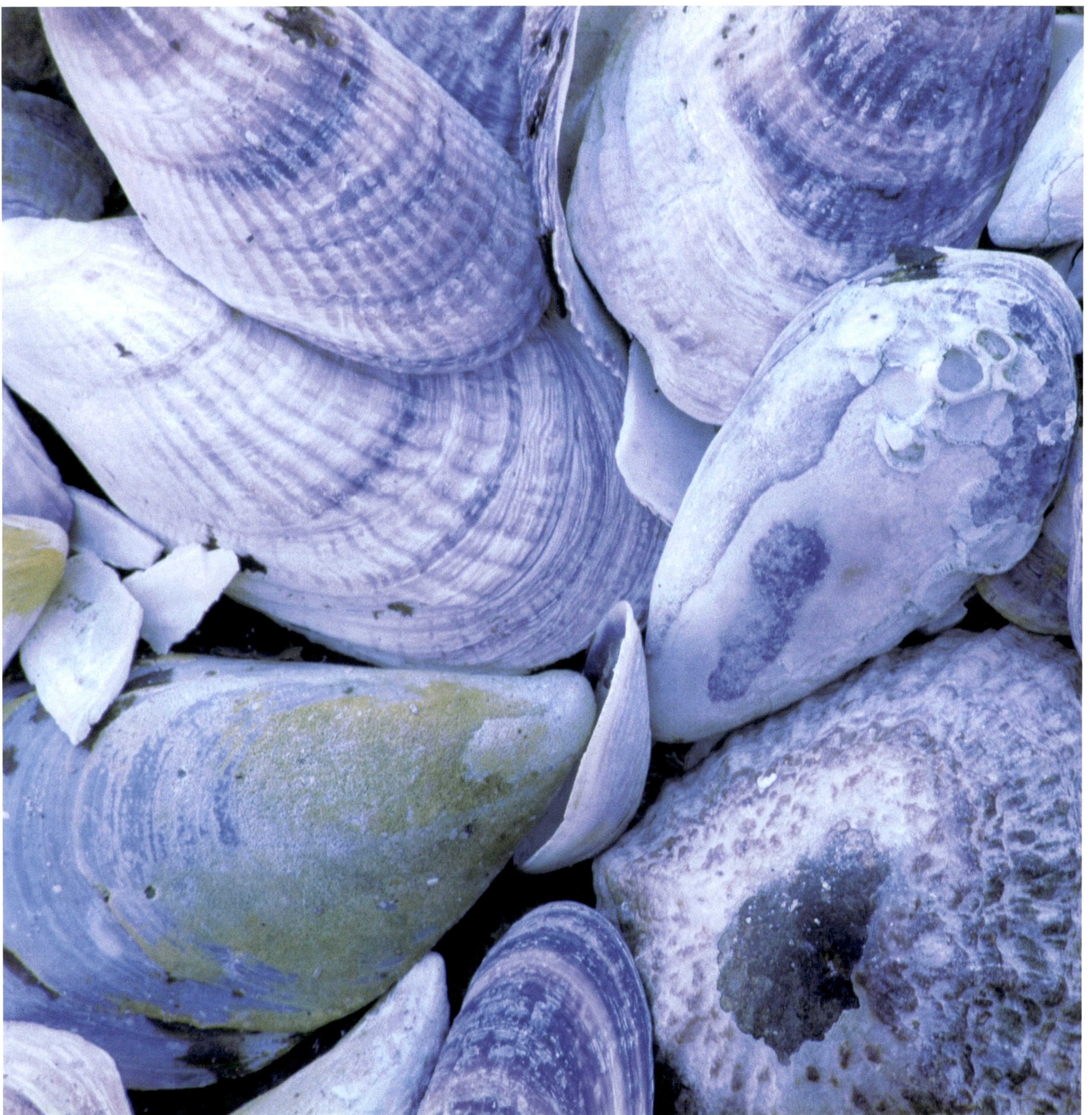

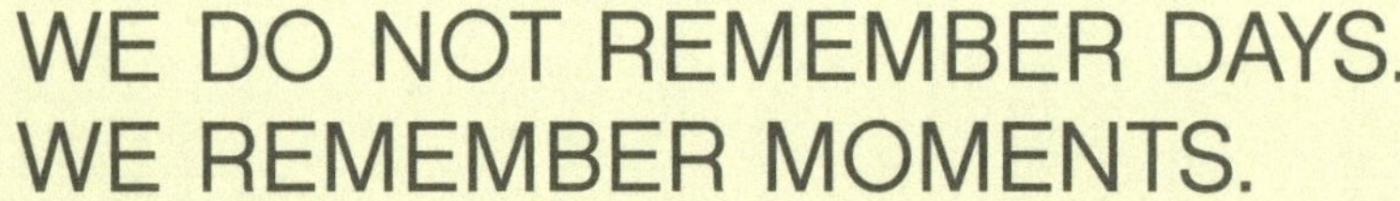

WE DO NOT REMEMBER DAYS.
WE REMEMBER MOMENTS.

CESARE PAVESE

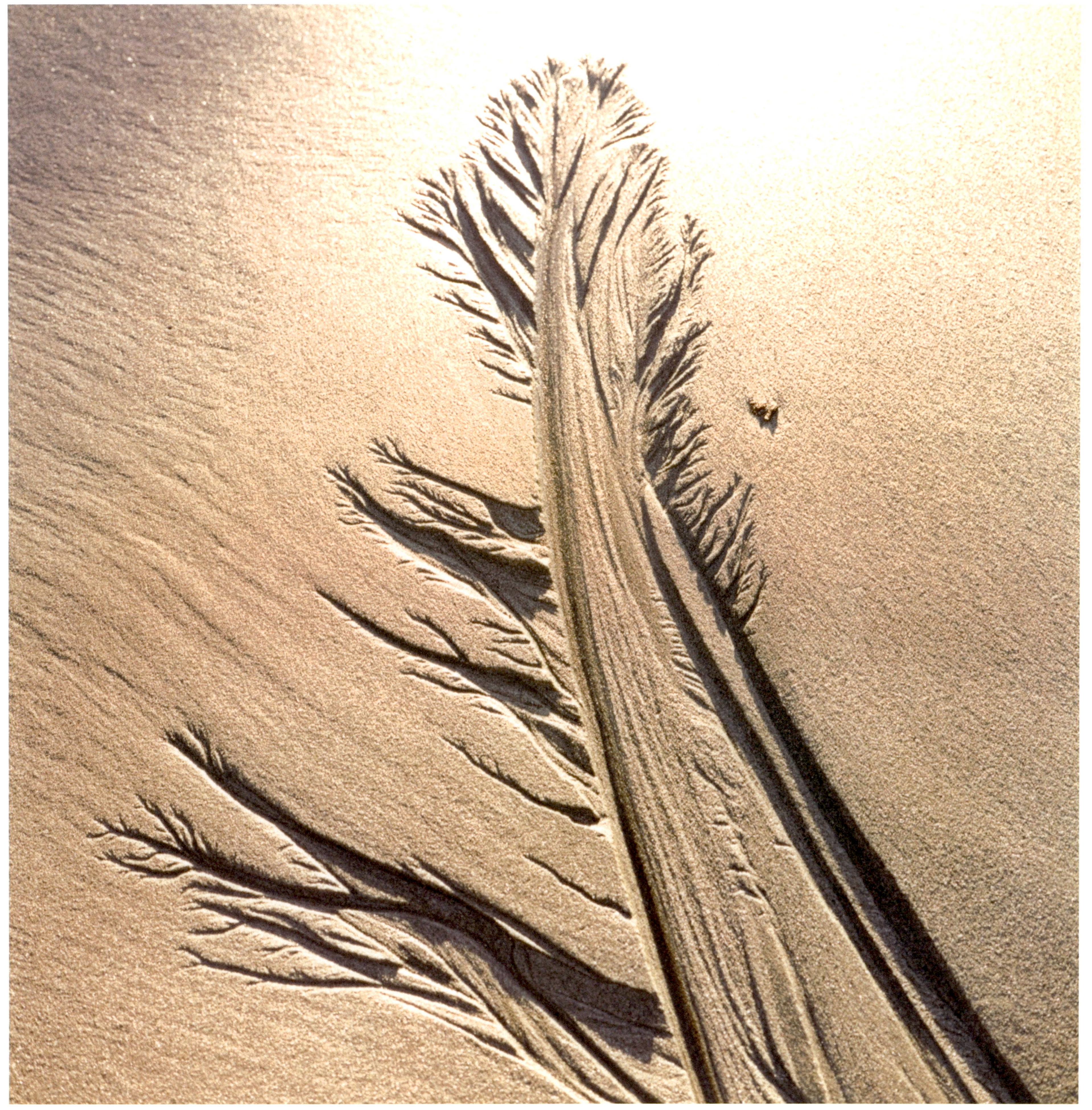

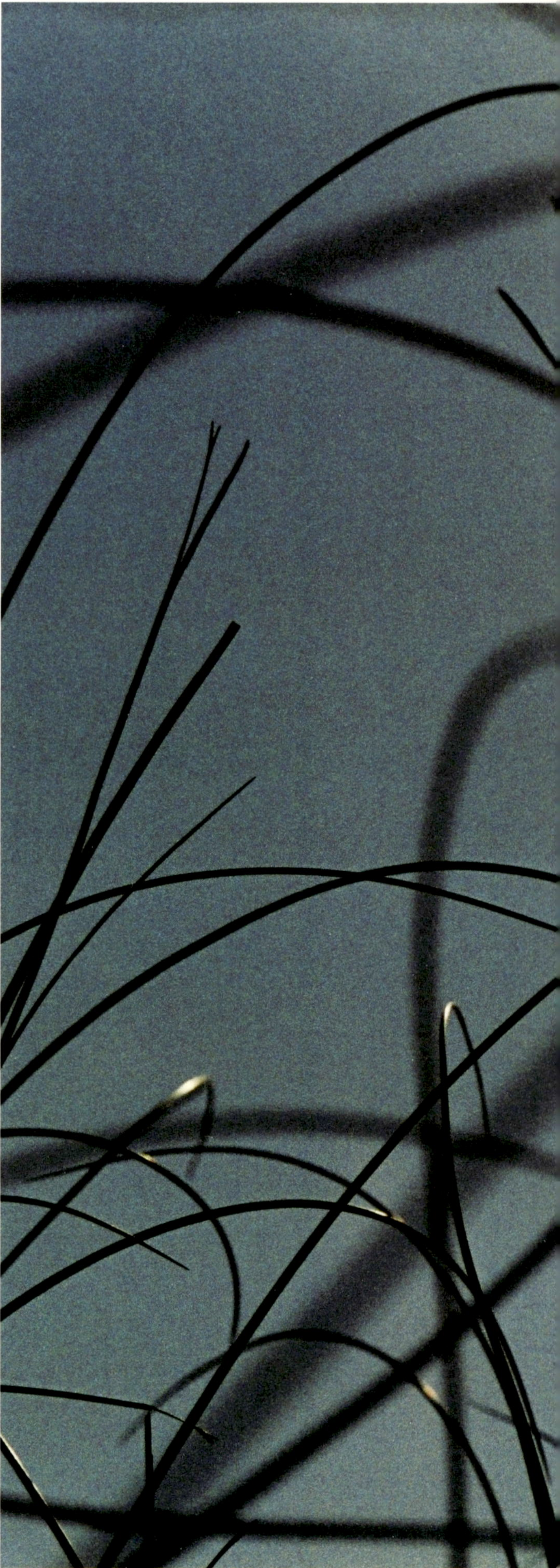

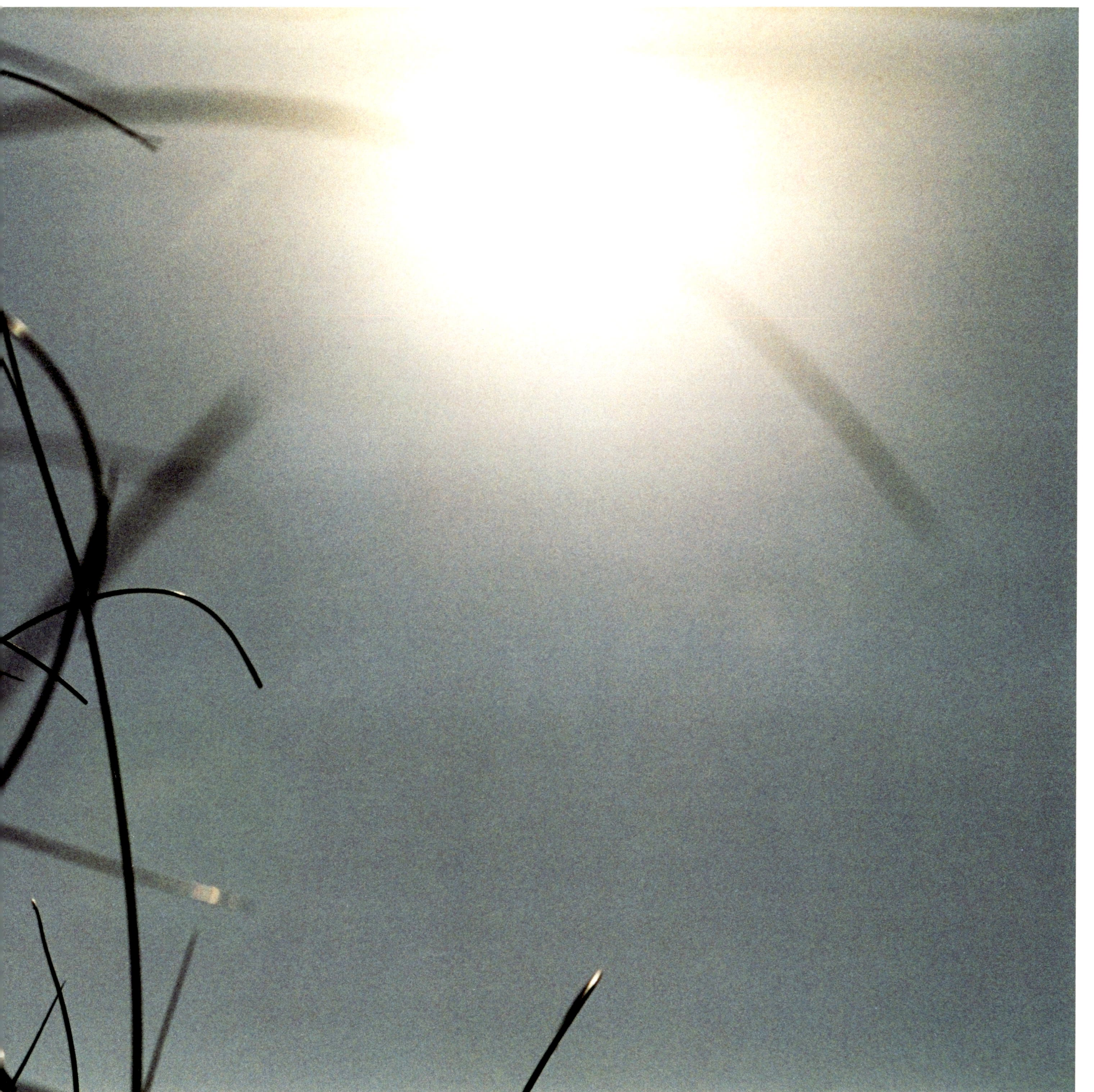

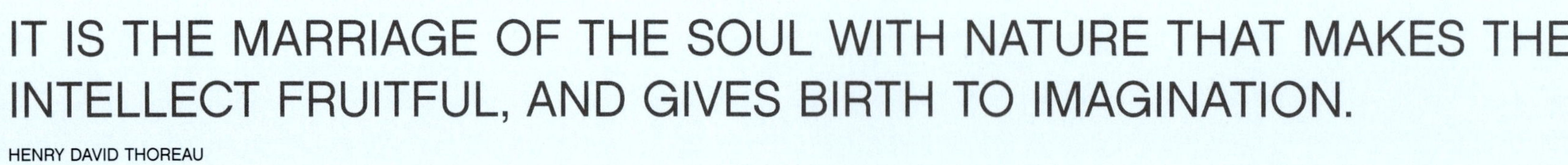

IT IS THE MARRIAGE OF THE SOUL WITH NATURE THAT MAKES THE
INTELLECT FRUITFUL, AND GIVES BIRTH TO IMAGINATION.
HENRY DAVID THOREAU

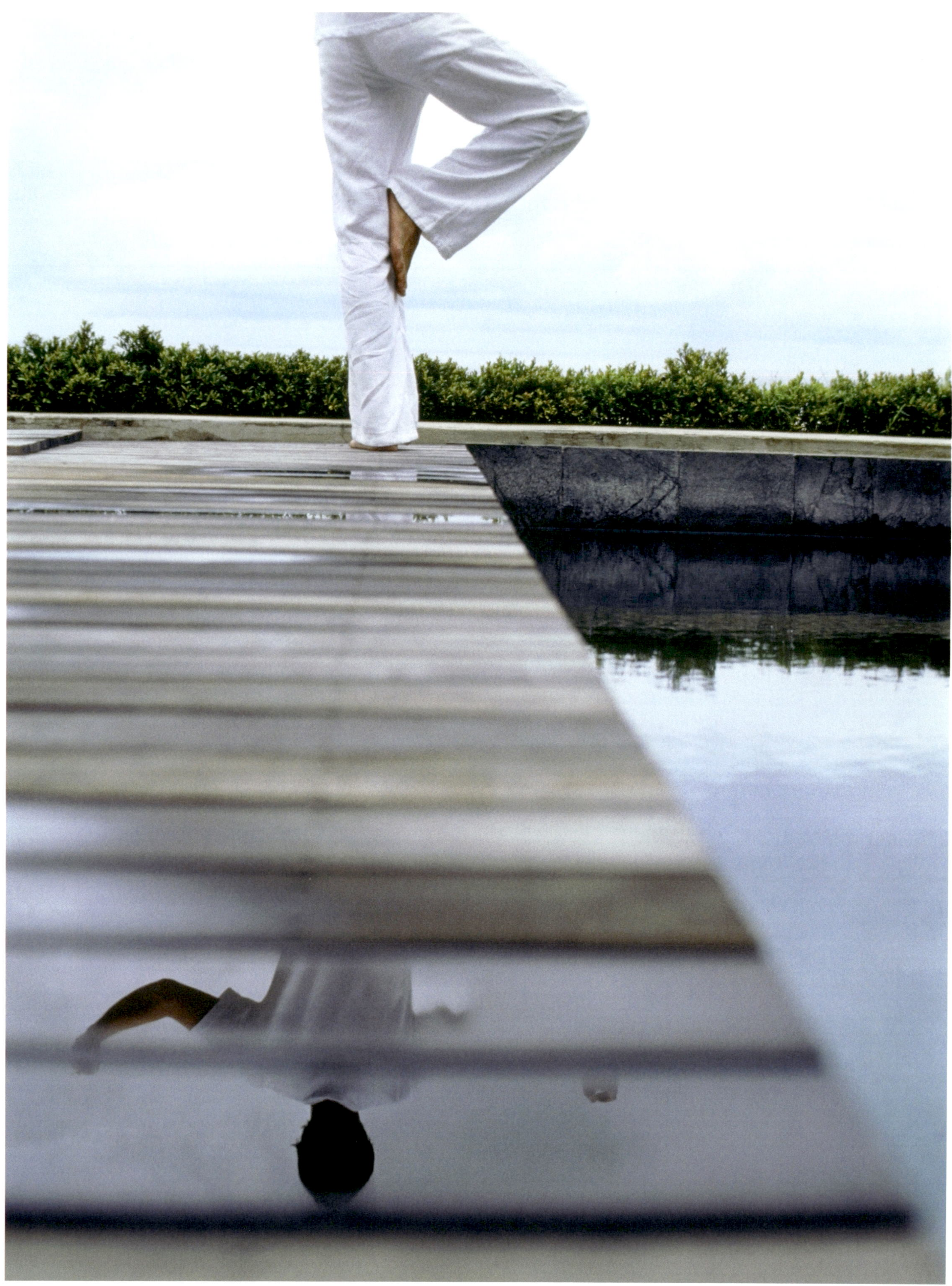

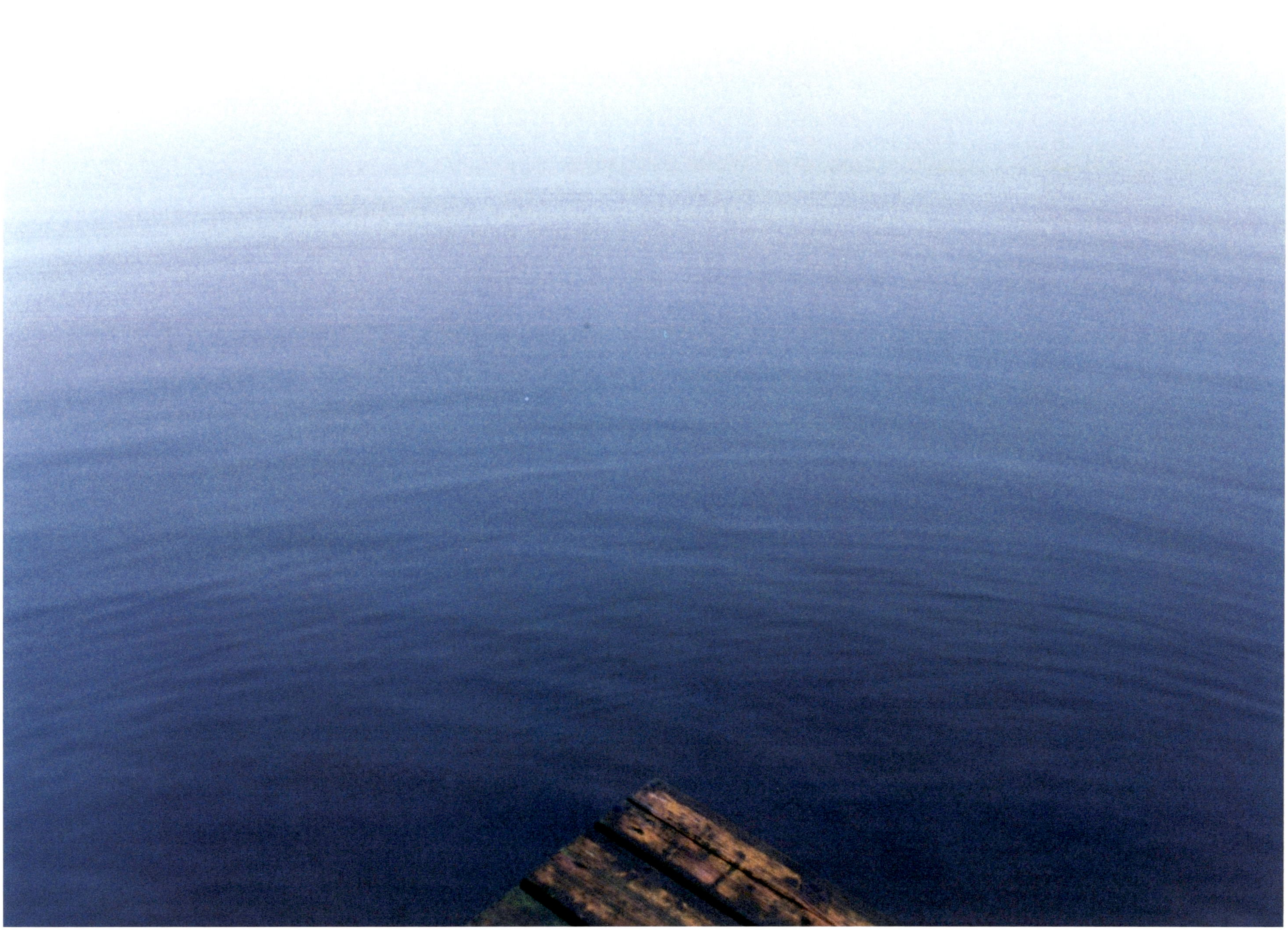

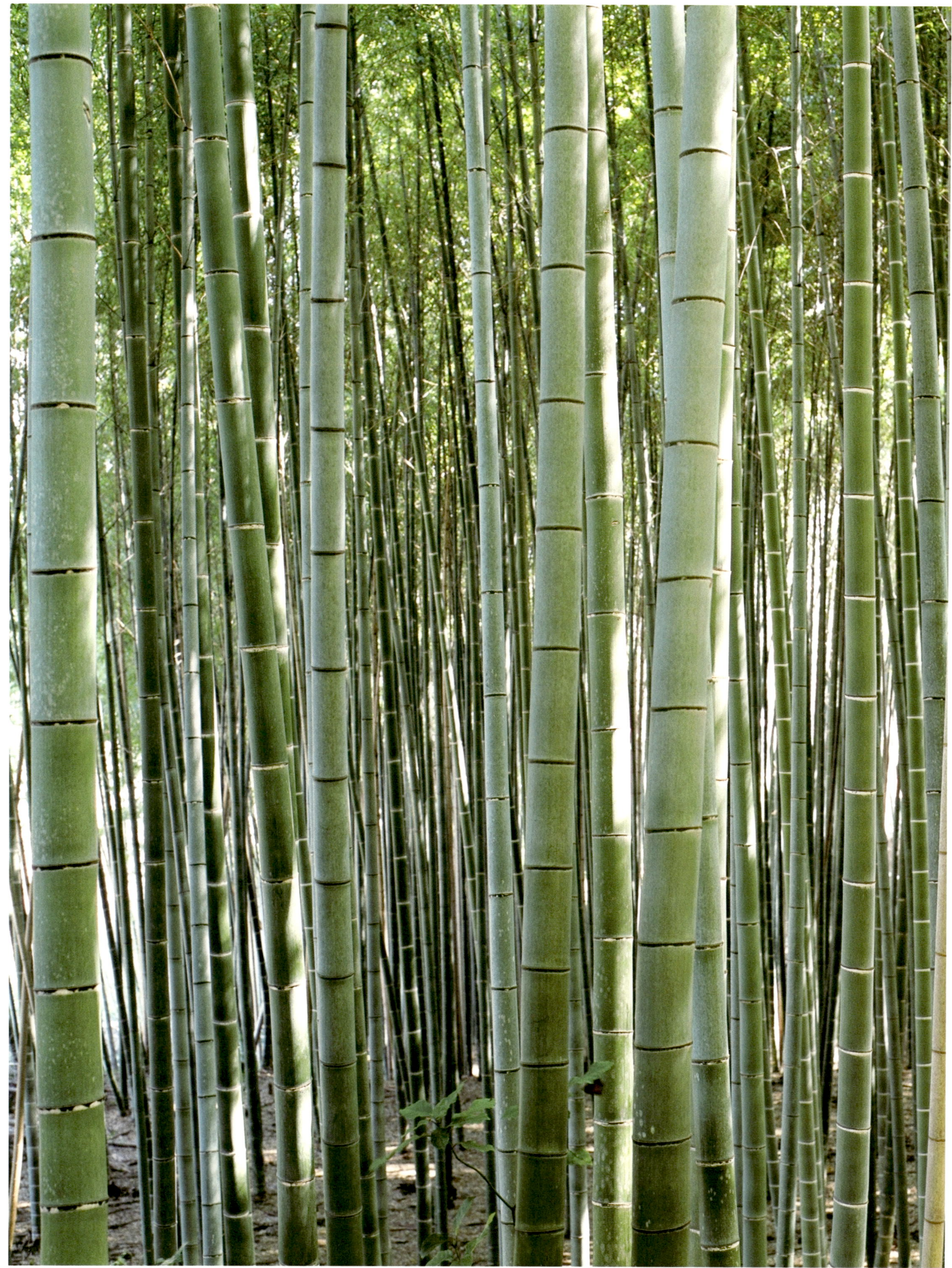

IF YOU SUCCEED IN ATTAINING INNER PEACE, THEN YOU
HAVE DONE MORE THAN SOMEONE WHO HAS CONQUERED
CITIES AND WHOLE EMPIRES.

MICHEL EYQUEM DE MONTAIGNE

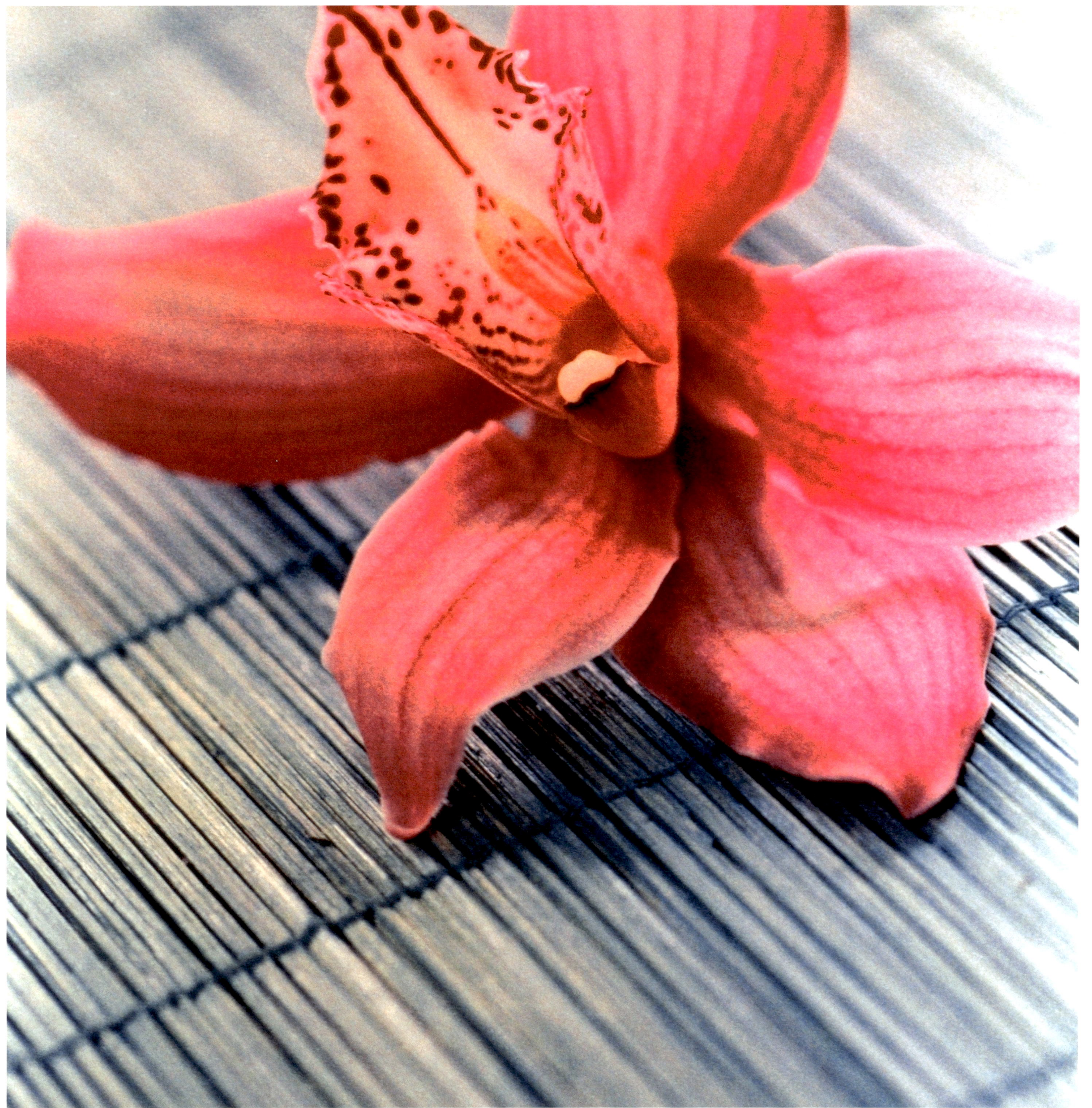

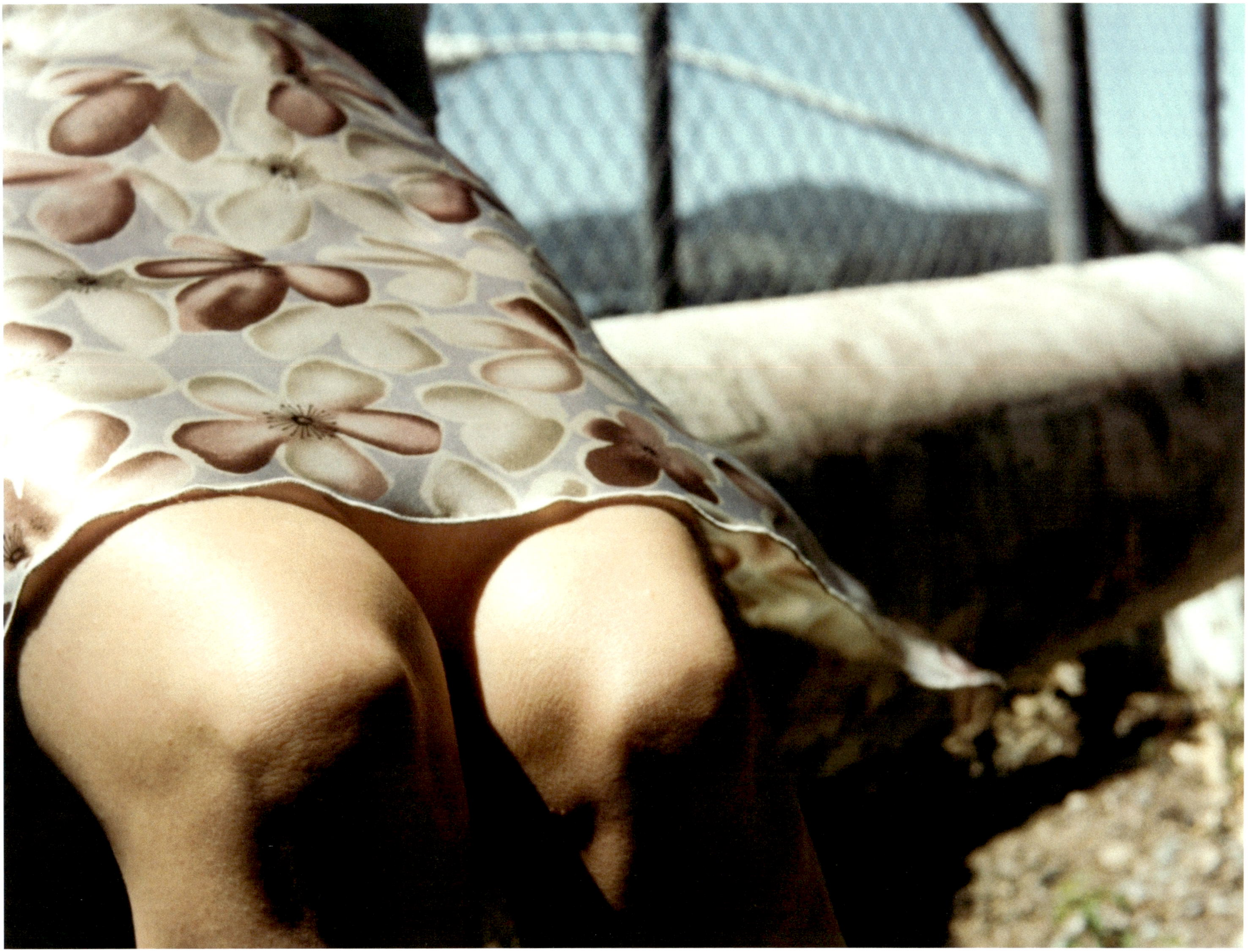

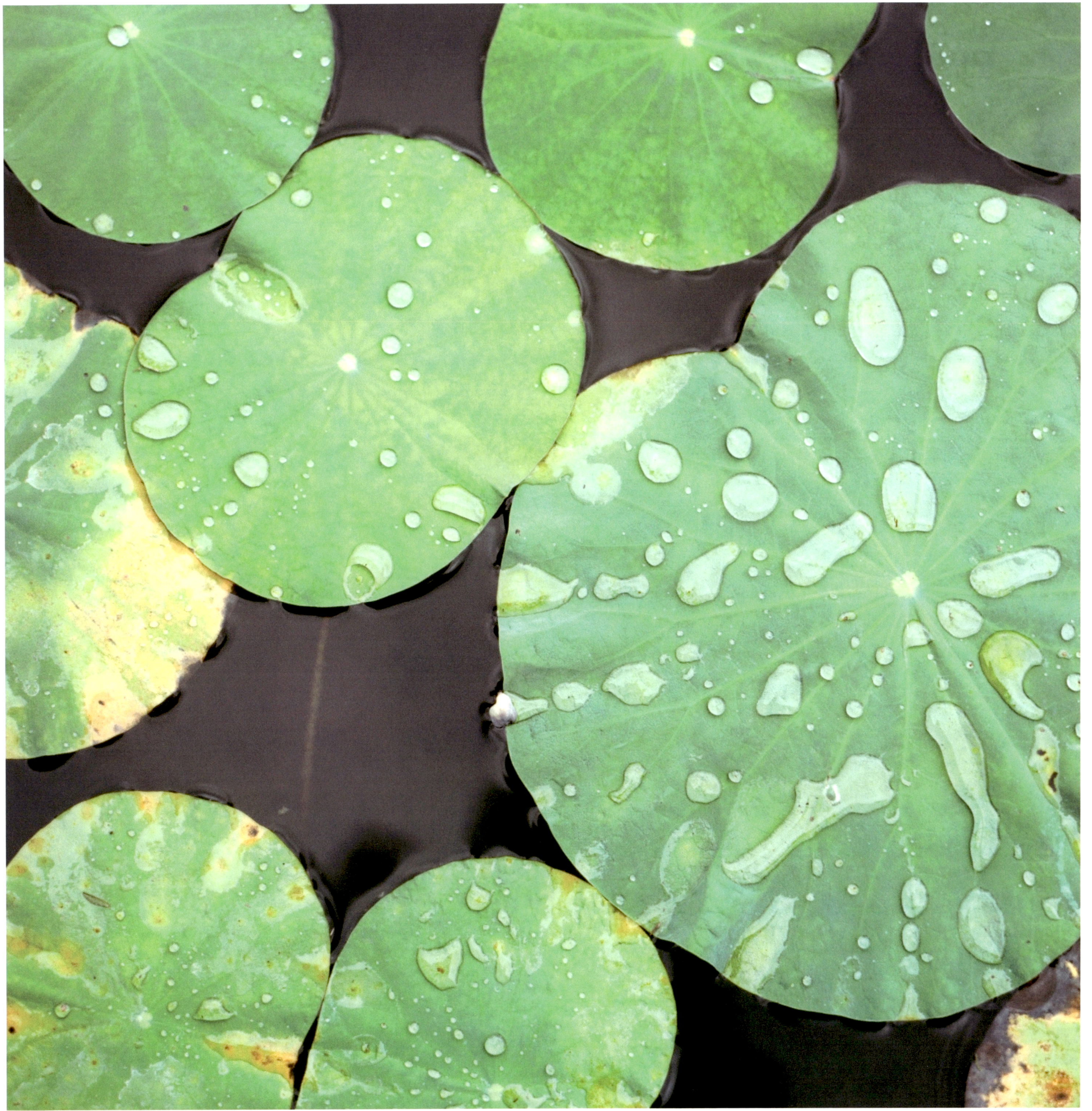

JUST AS THE LEVEL OF THE WATER CANNOT BE ALTERED AT ONE PLACE IN A LAKE AND NOT AT OTHERS, OUR HAPPINESS CANNOT BE INCREASED OR DECREASED BY MATERIAL POSSESSIONS.

LEO N. TOLSTOY

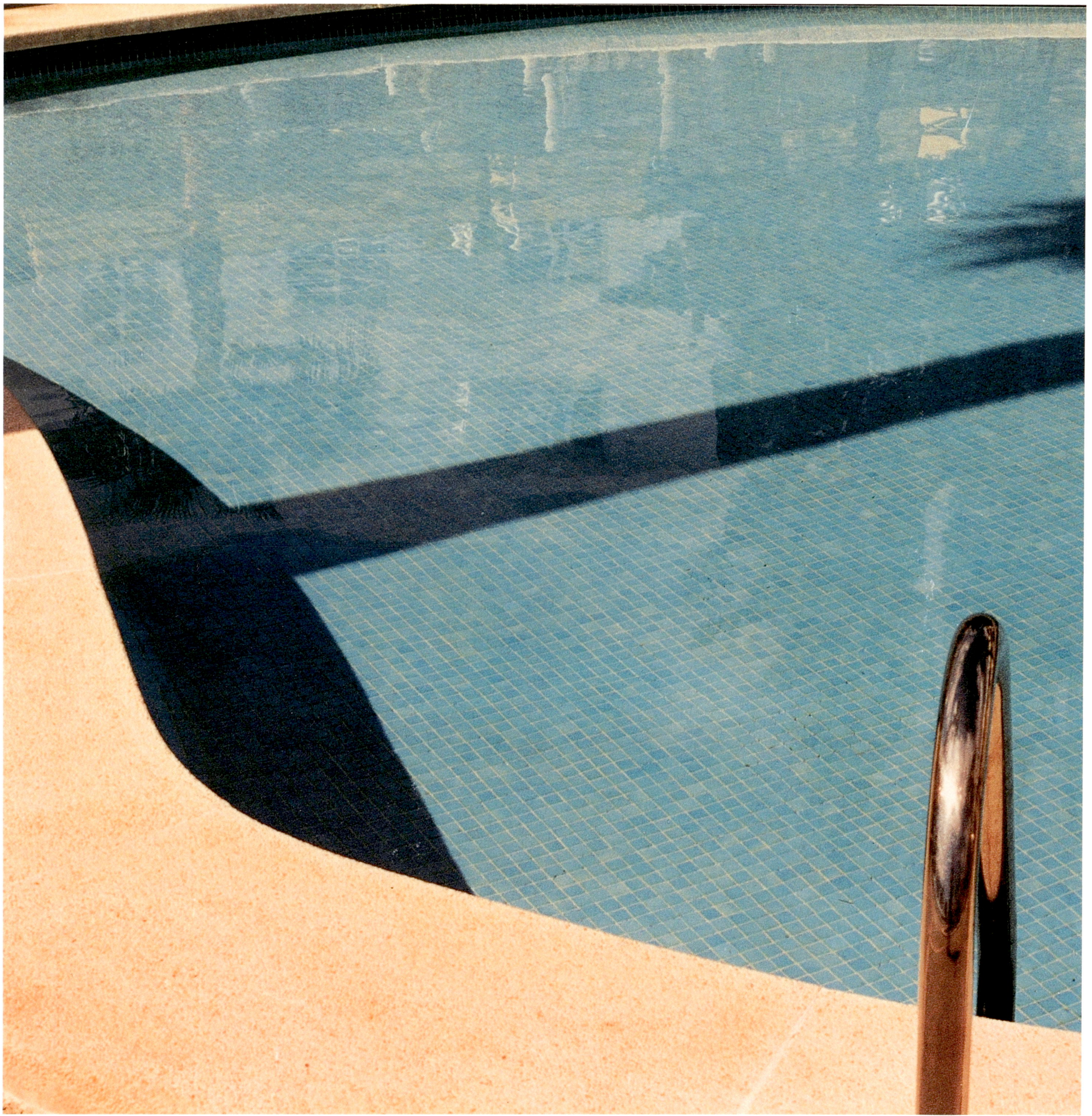

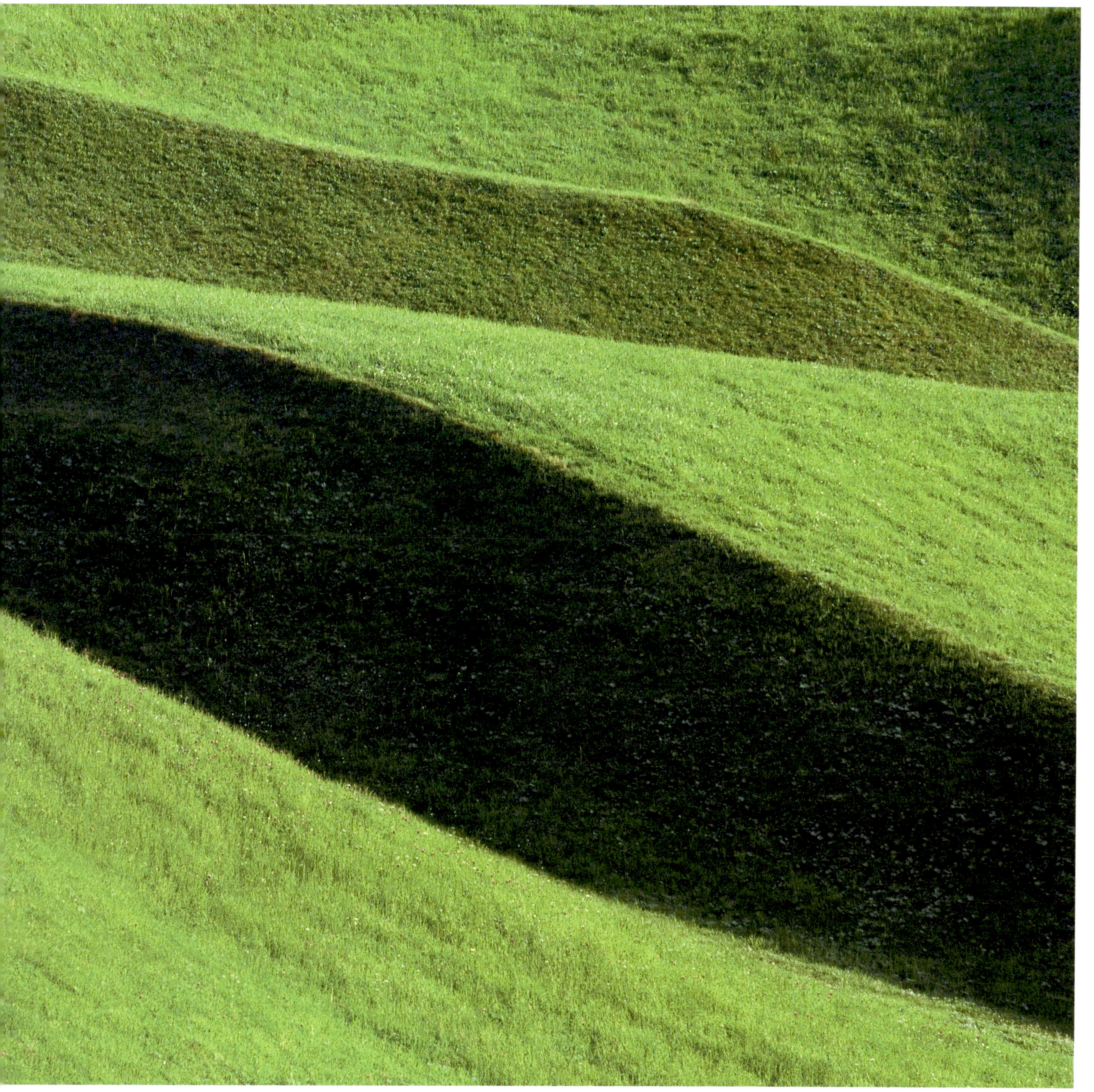

UNDERSTANDING – THROUGH PEACE.
WORK – THROUGH PEACE.
WIN – IN PEACE.

DAG HAMMARSKJÖLD

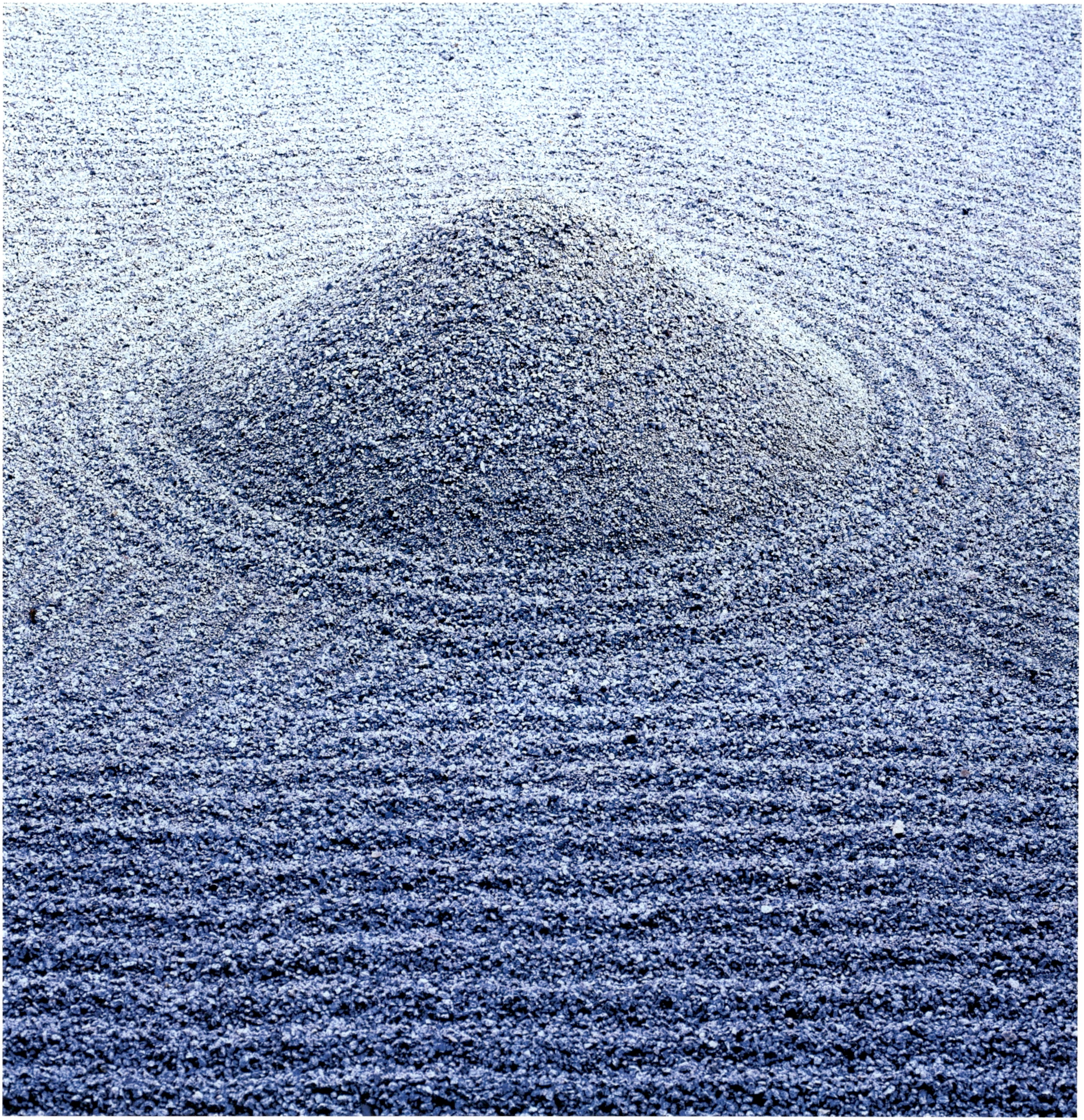

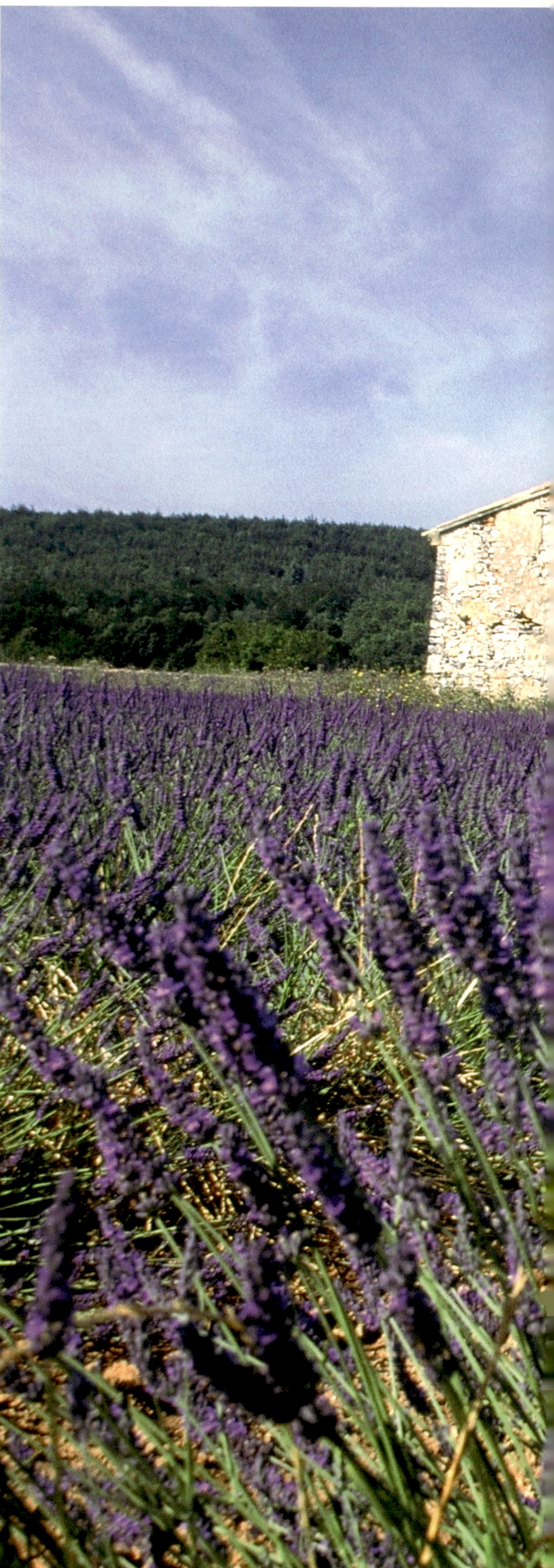

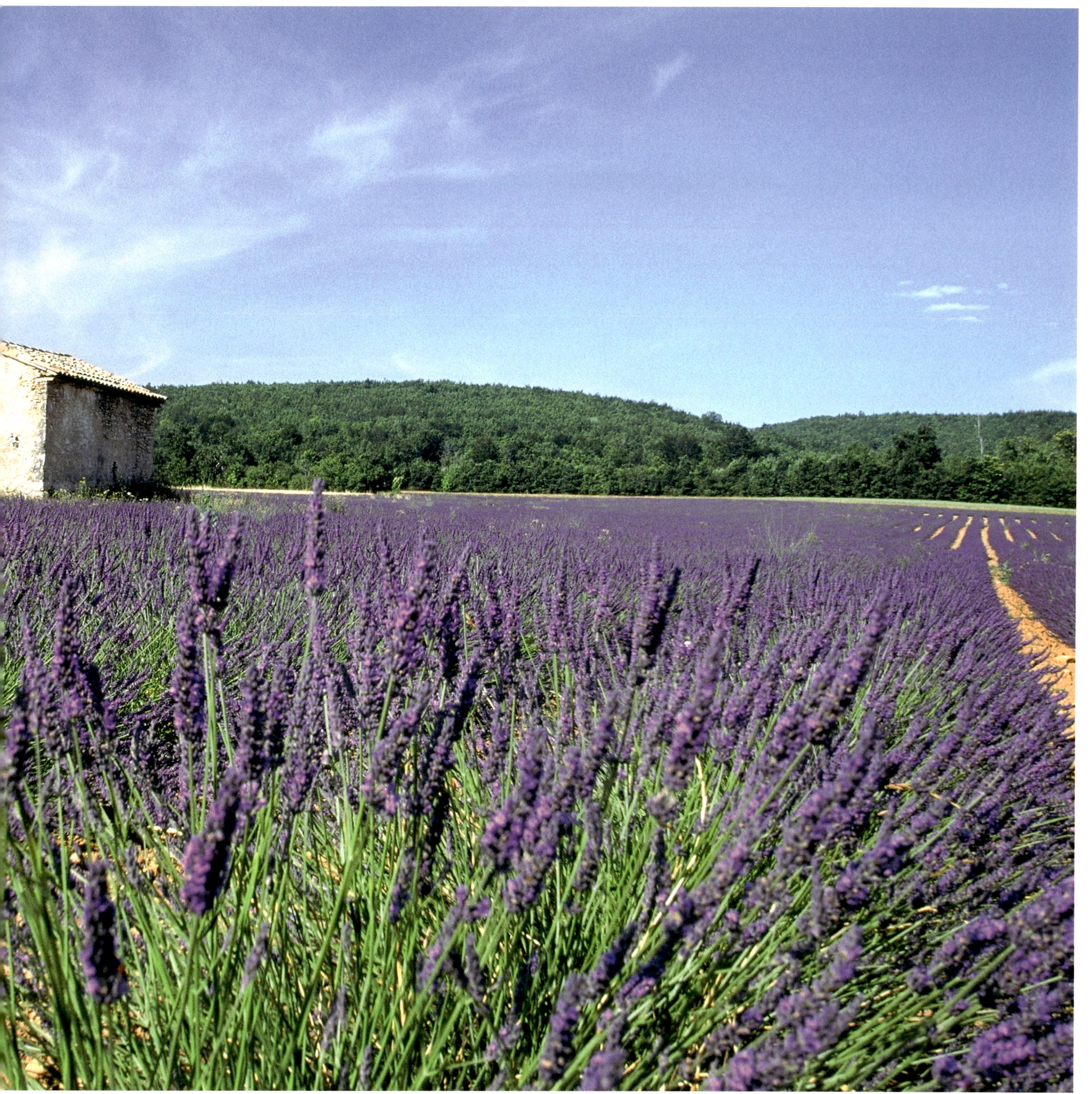

THE MOMENT ONE GIVES CLOSE ATTENTION TO ANYTHING,
EVEN A BLADE OF GRASS, IT BECOMES A MYSTERIOUS, AWESOME,
INDESCRIBABLY MAGNIFICENT WORLD IN ITSELF.

HENRY MILLER

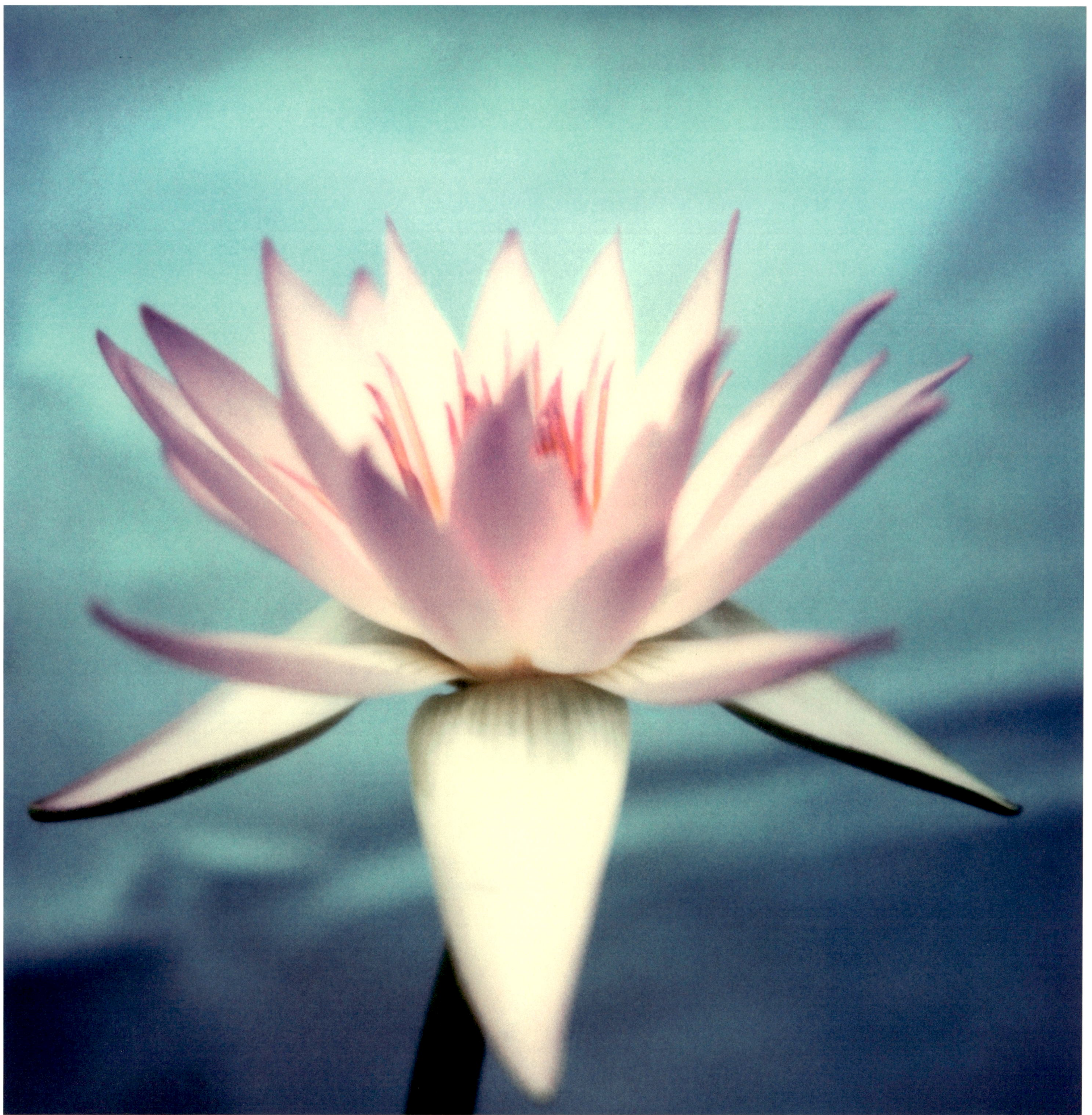

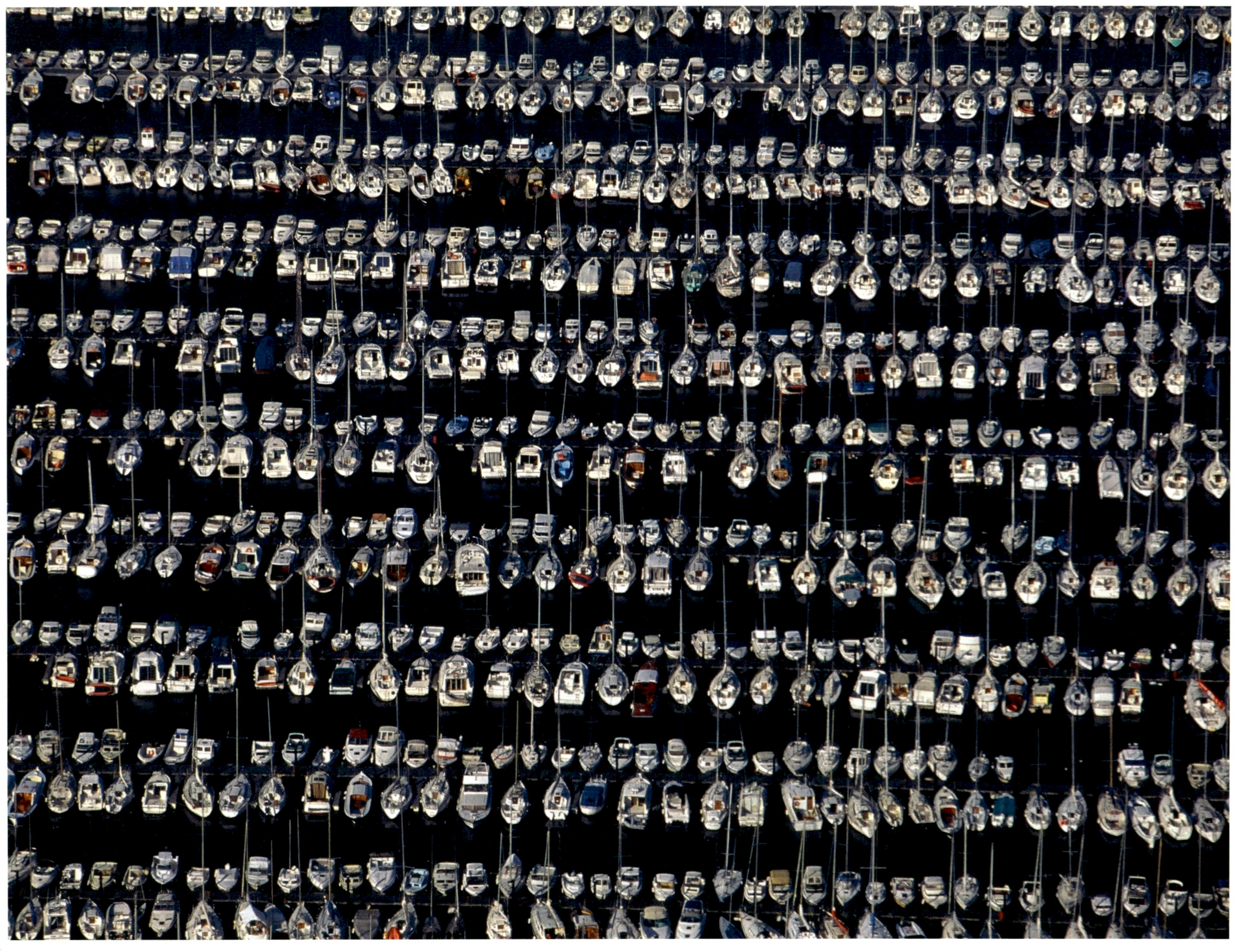

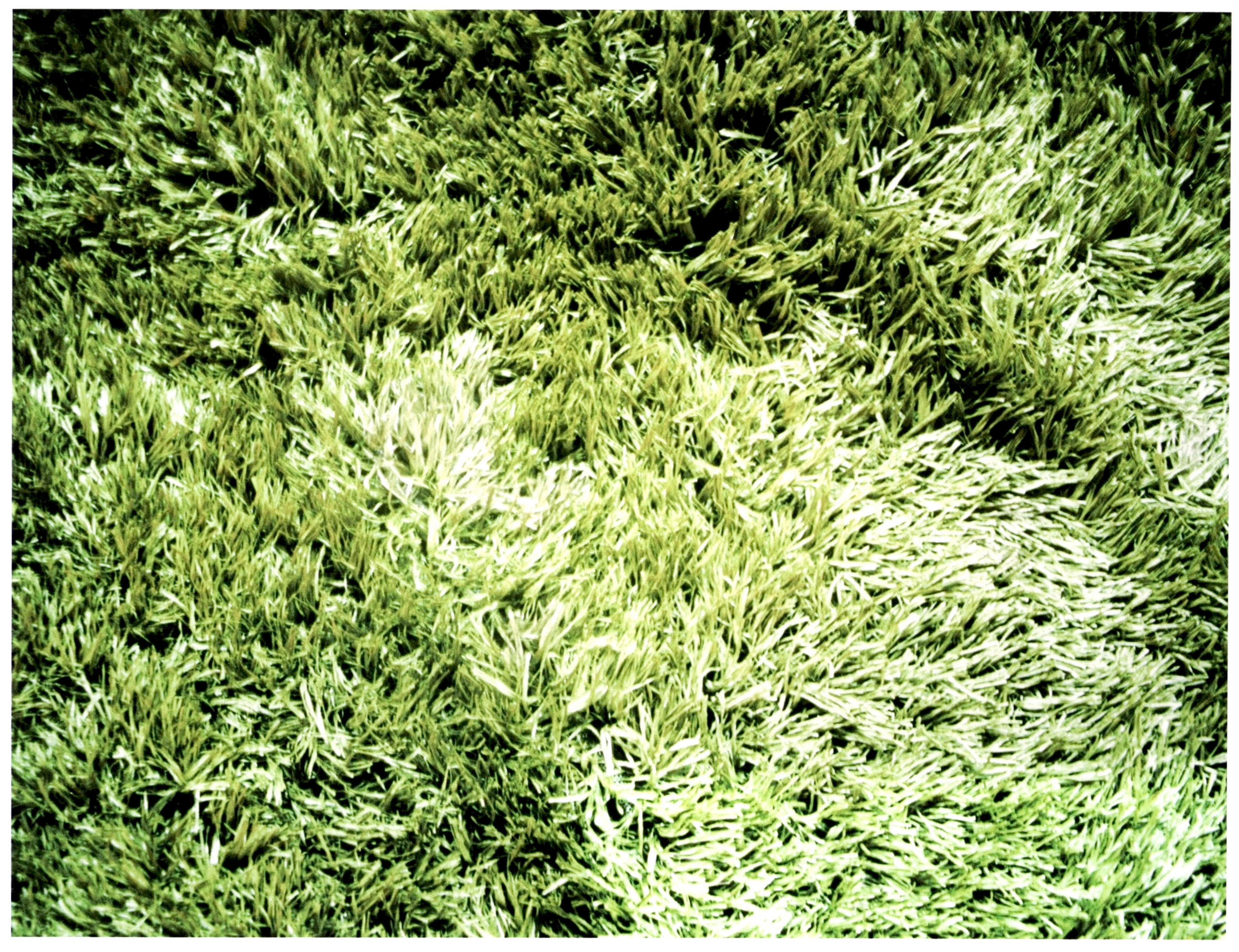

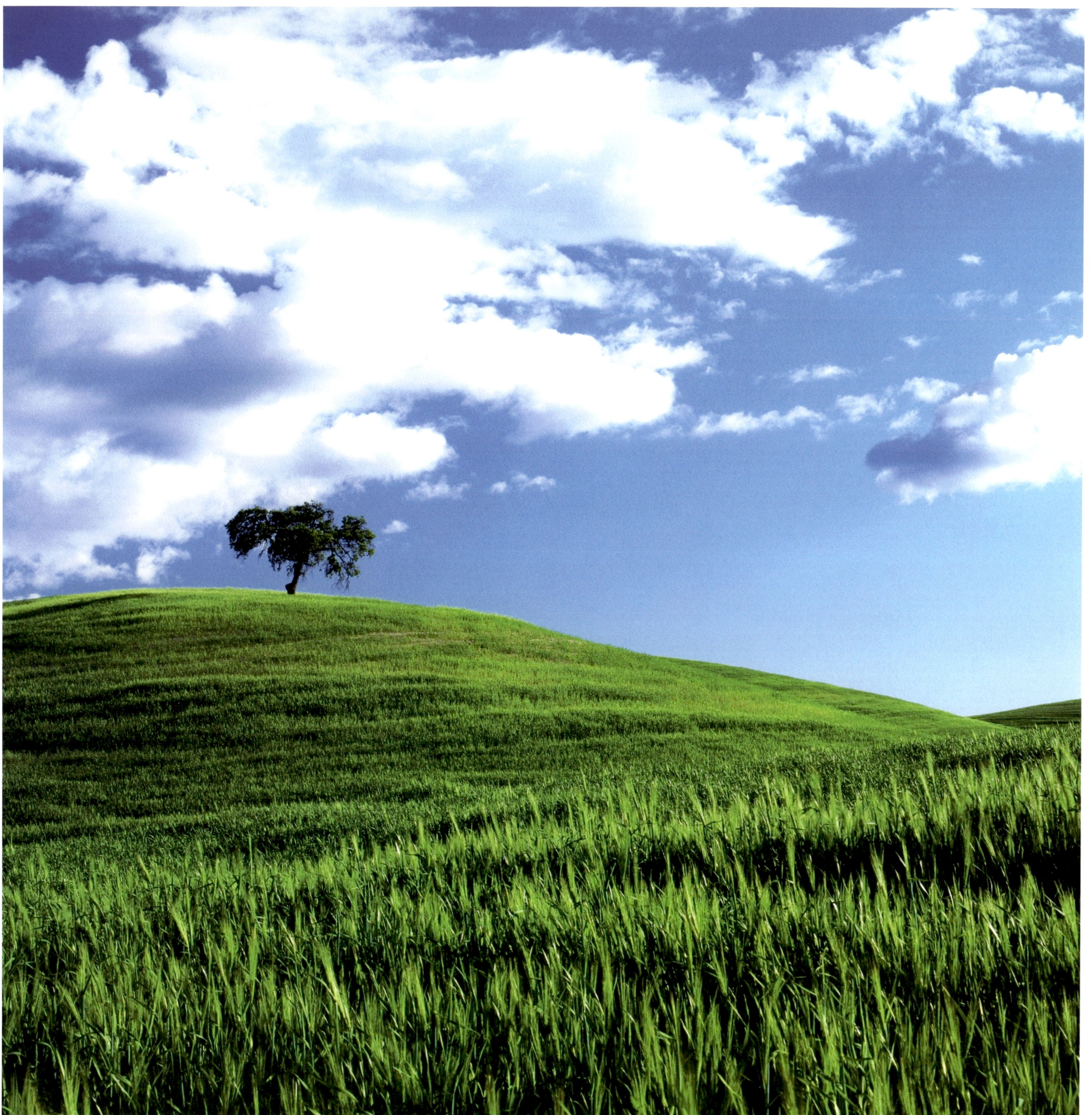

ONLY PEACE IS THE SOURCE
OF EVERY GREAT POWER.
FYODOR M. DOSTOYEWSKY

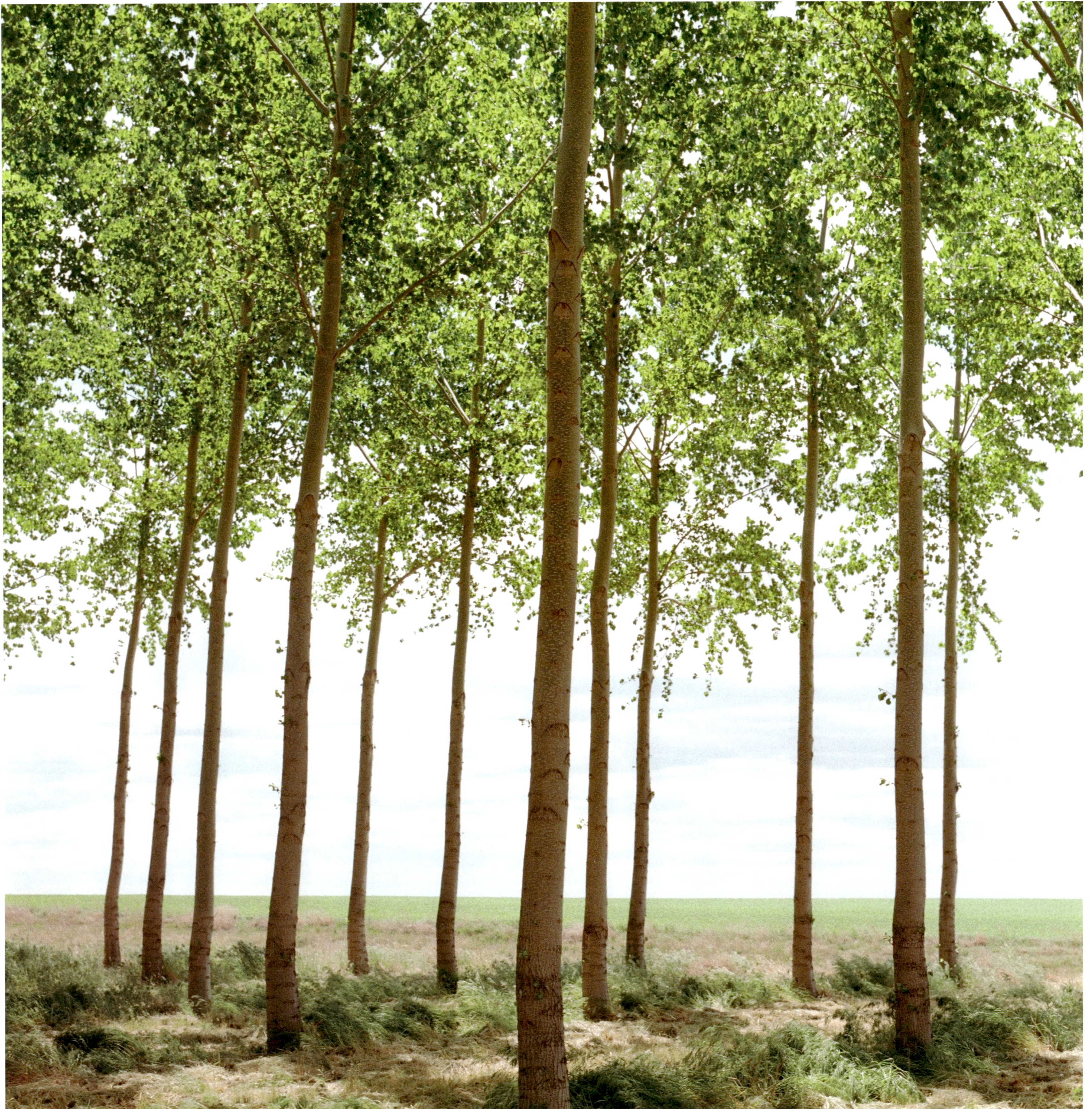

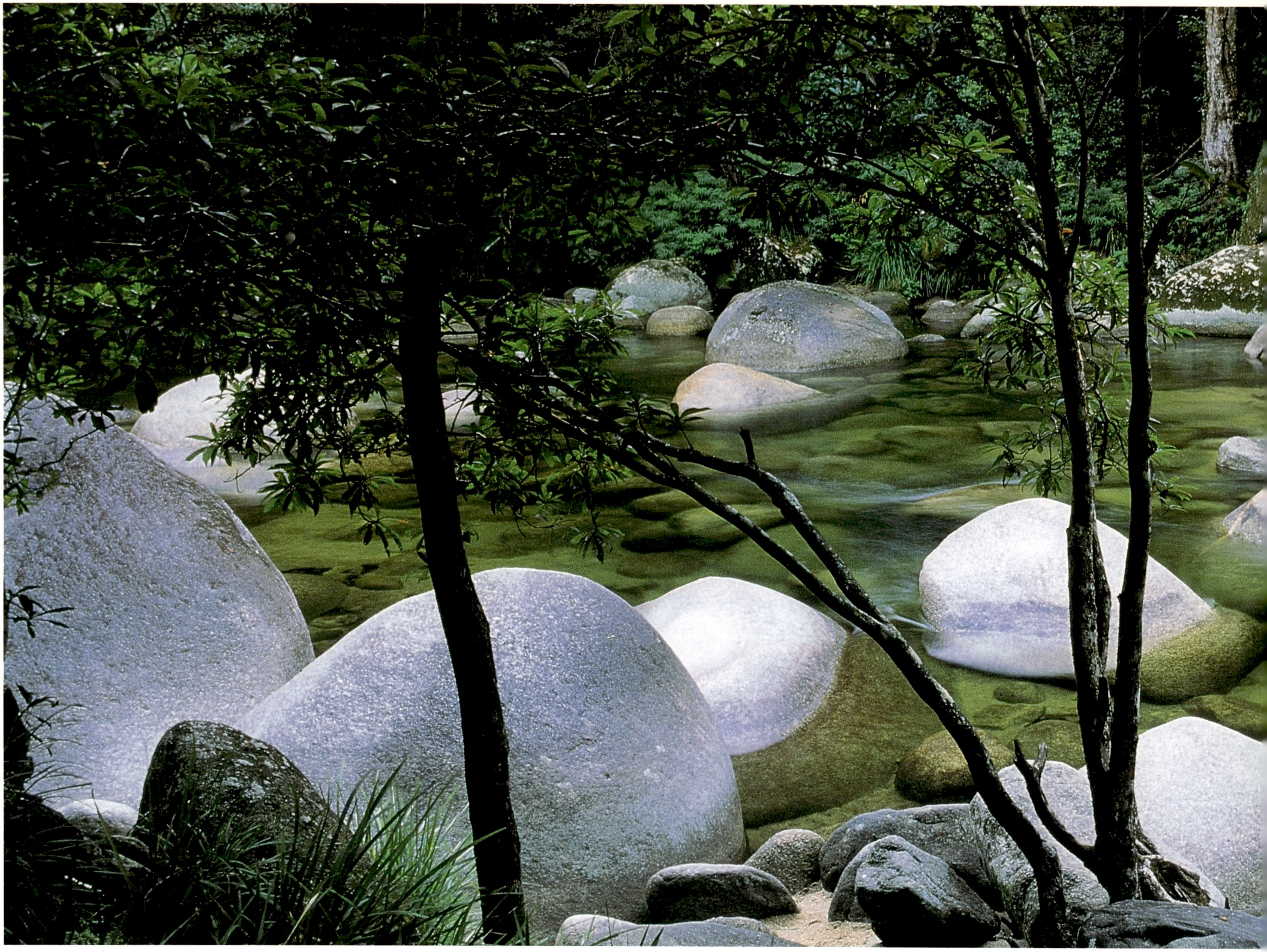

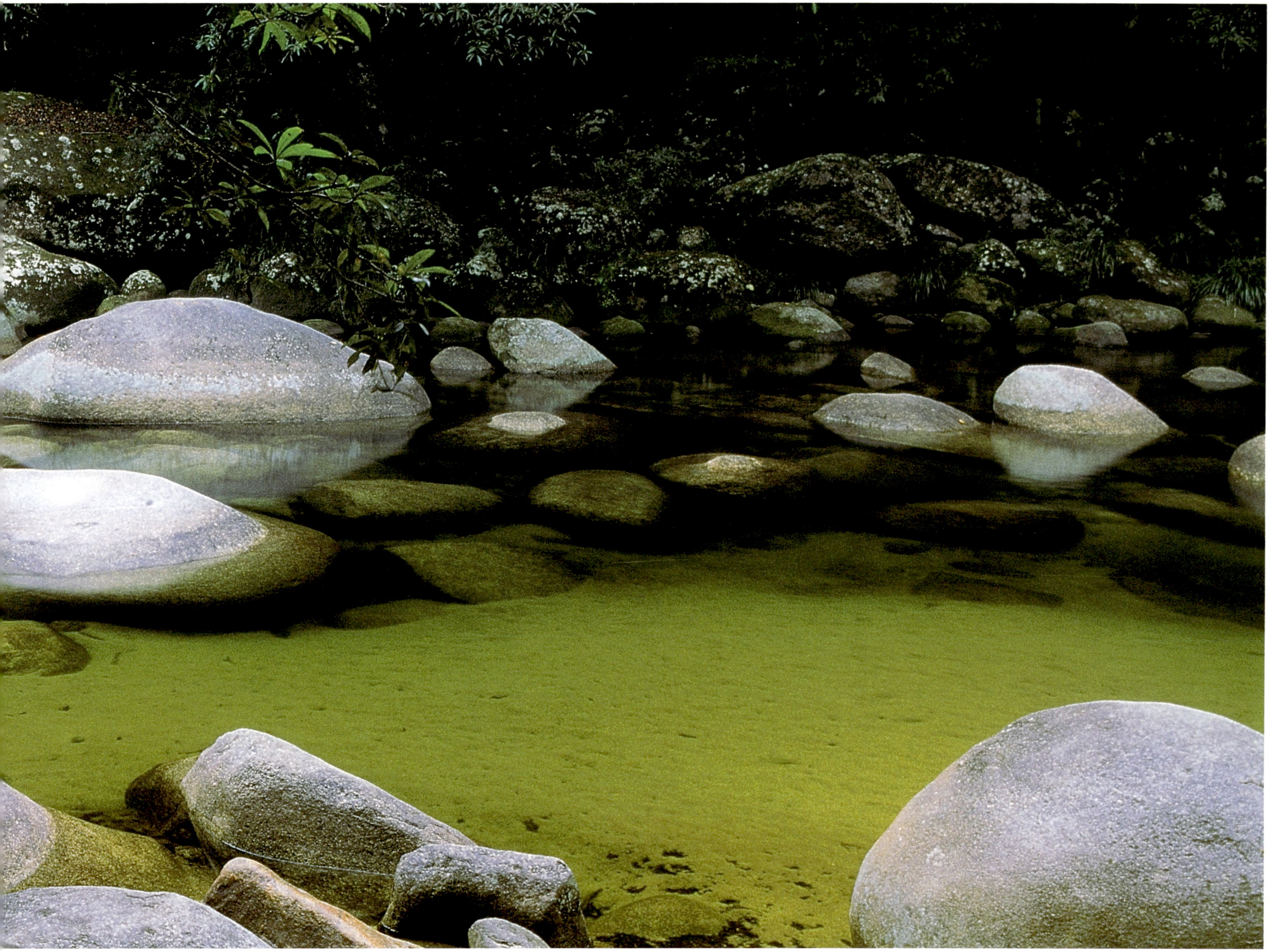

IT'S THE LITTLE THINGS THAT MAKE
LIFE COMPLETE.

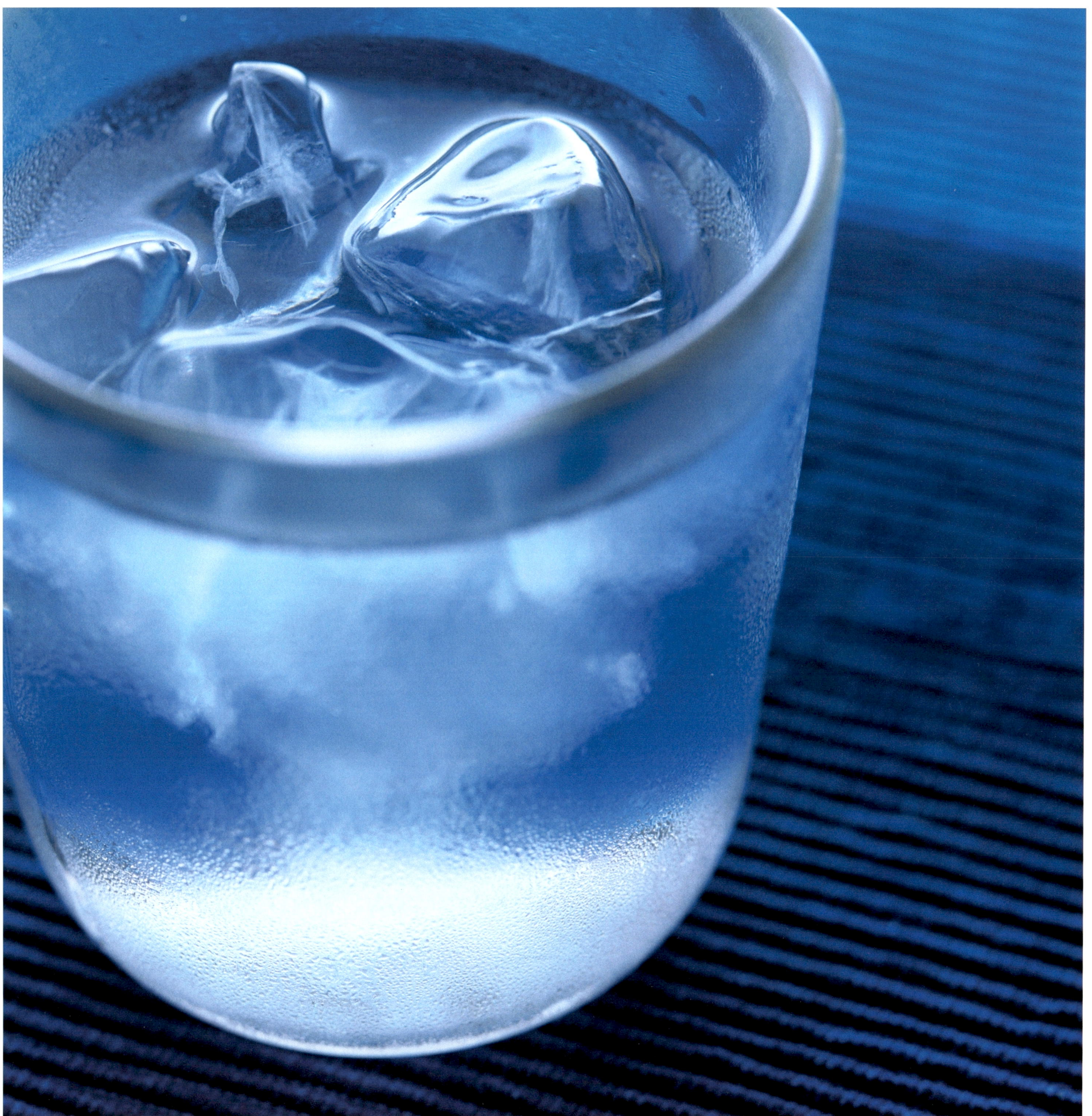

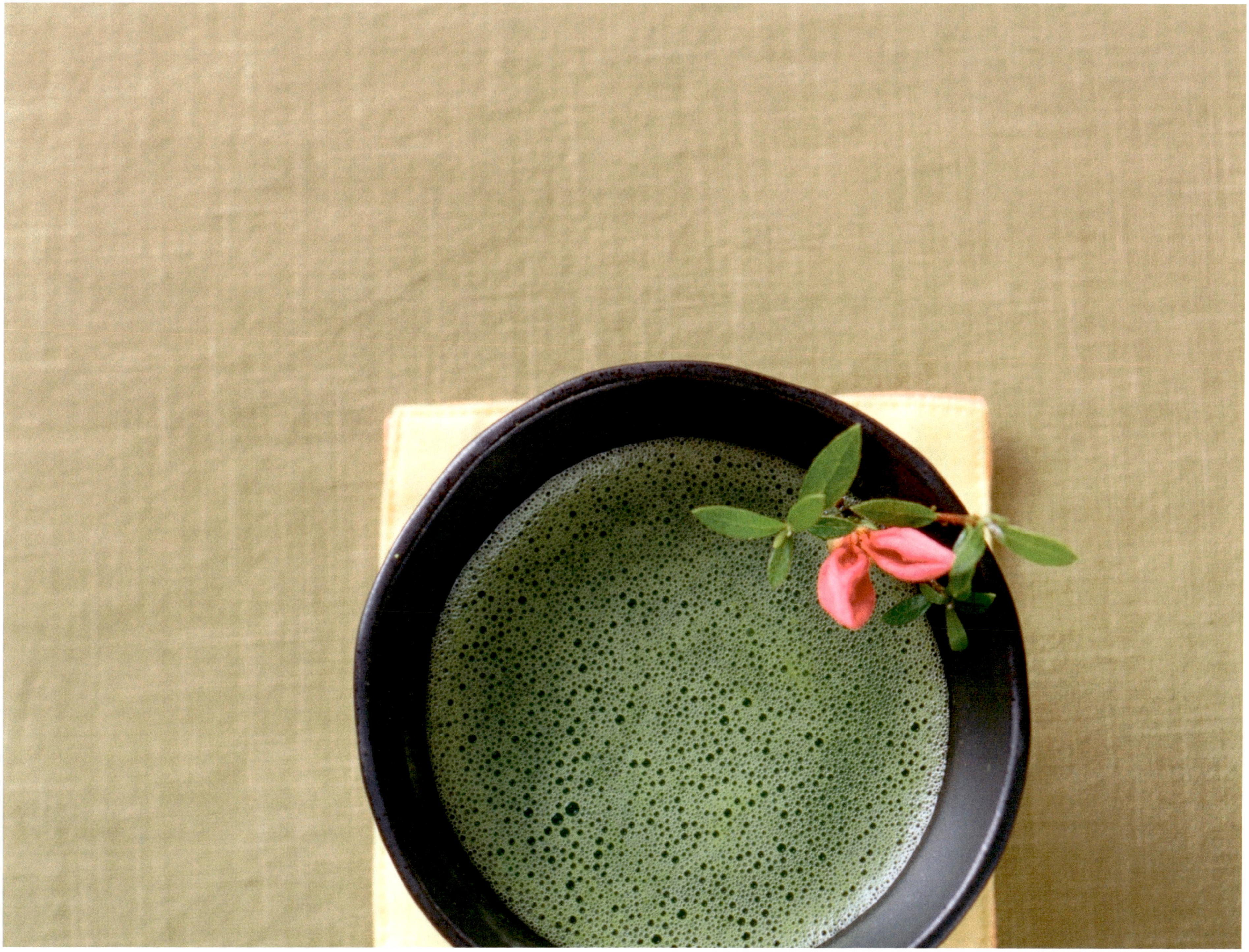

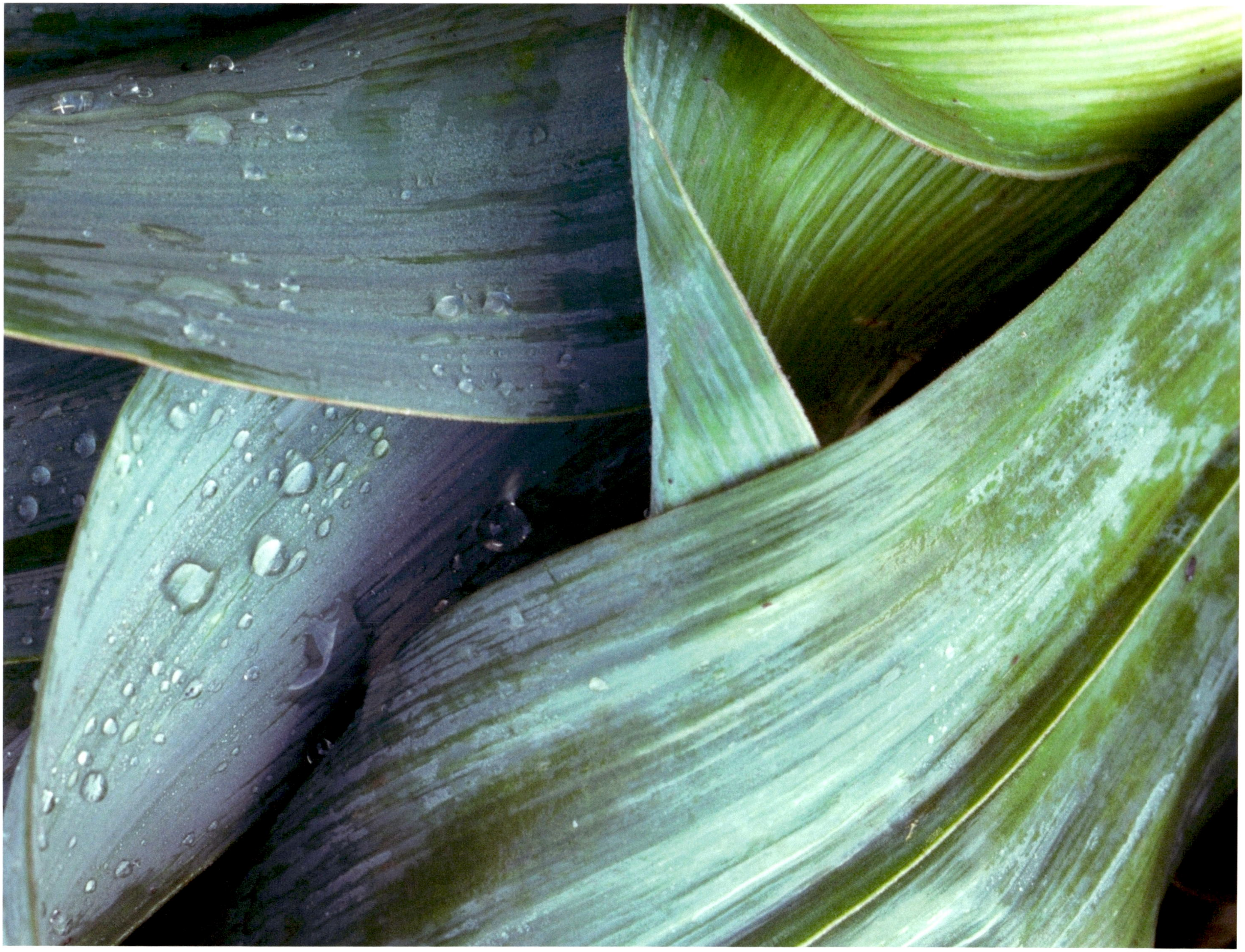

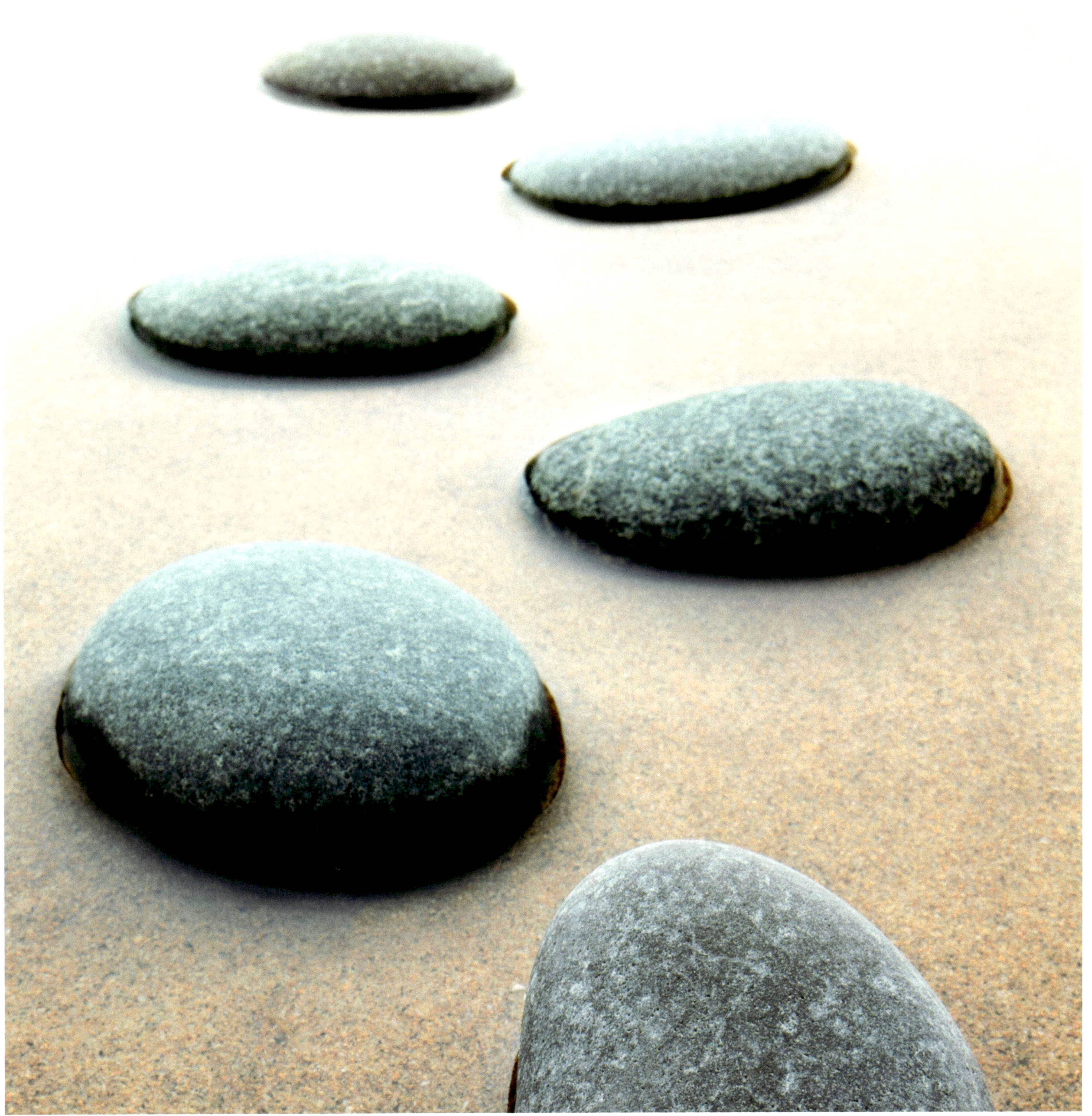

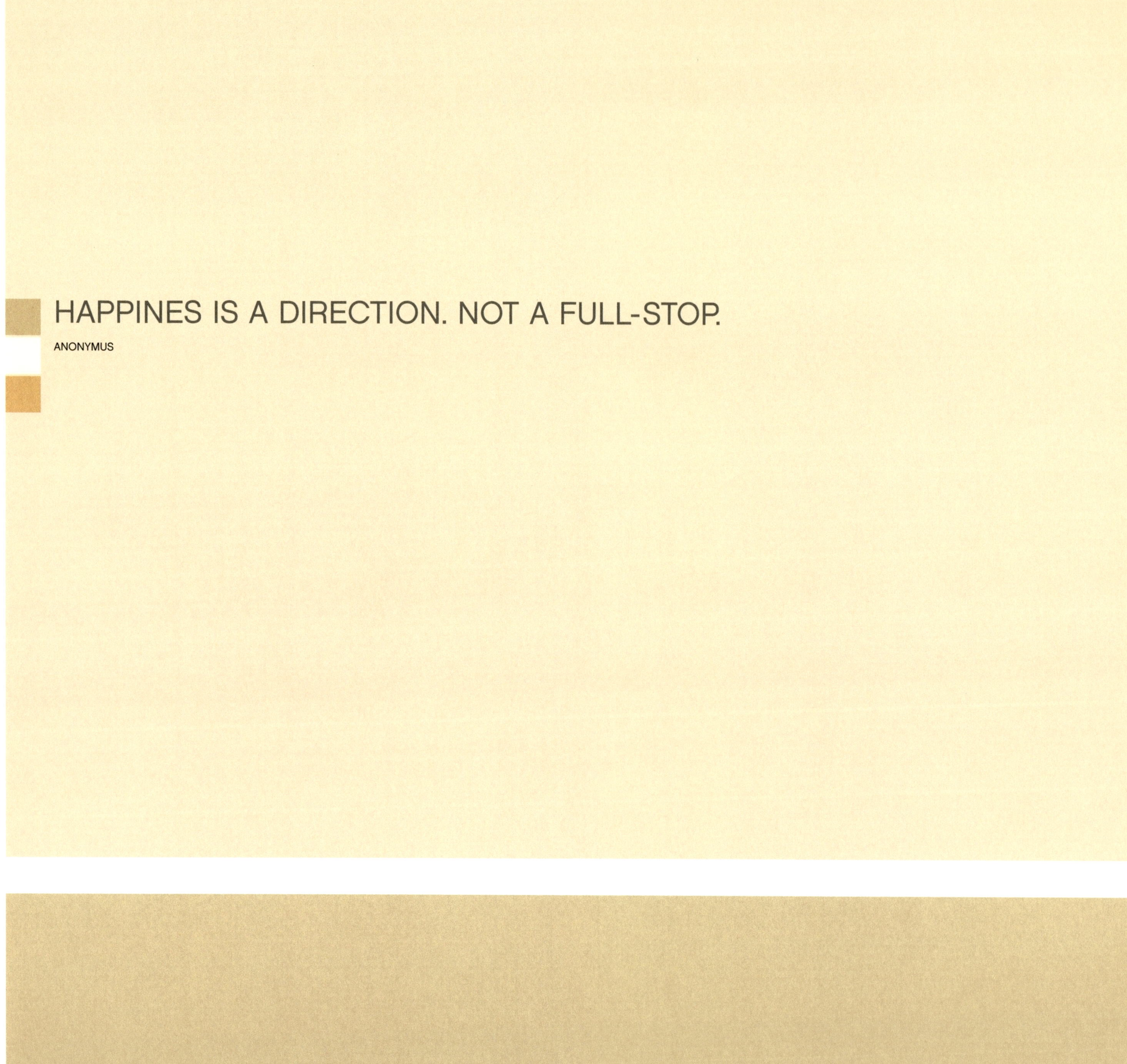
HAPPINES IS A DIRECTION. NOT A FULL-STOP.
ANONYMUS

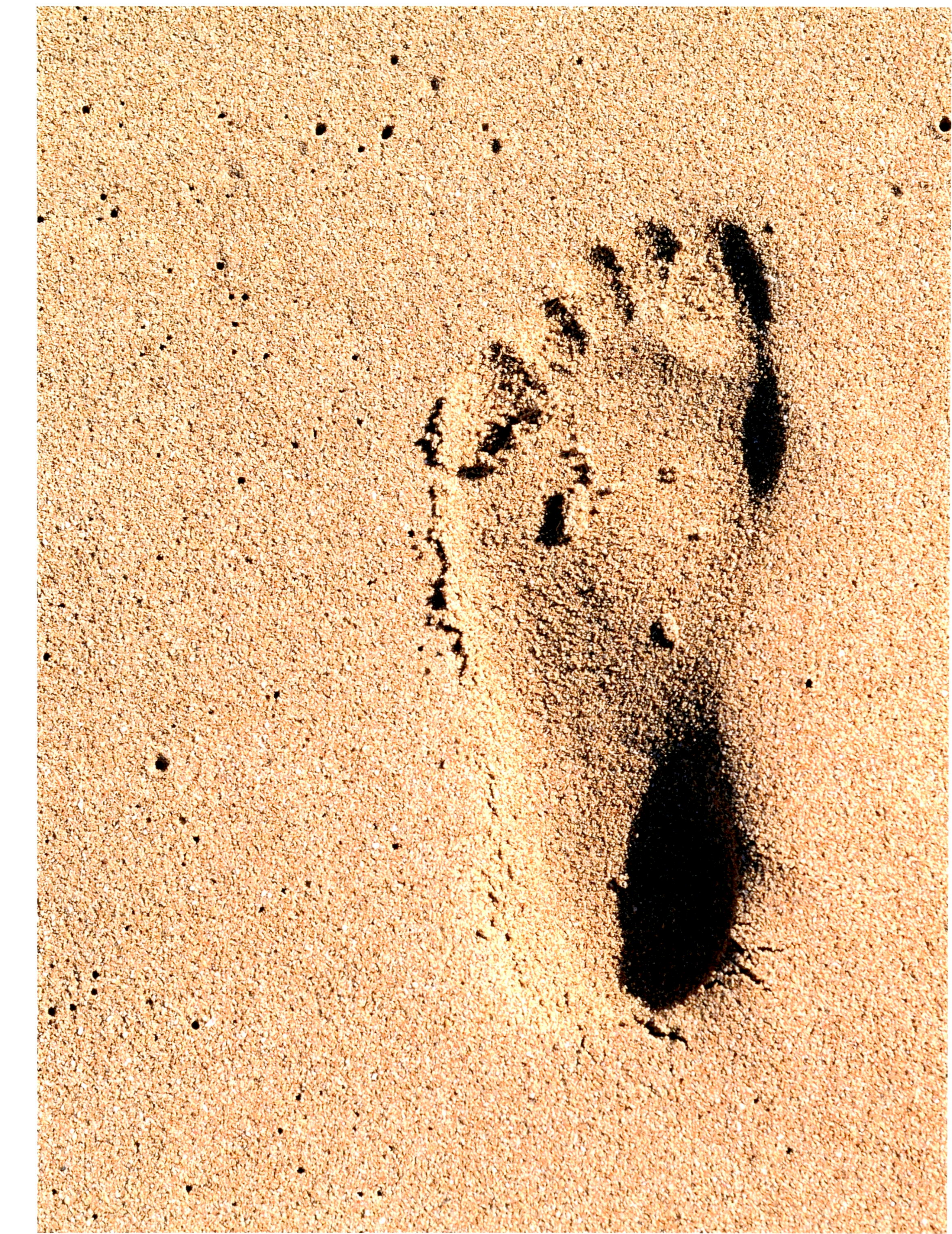

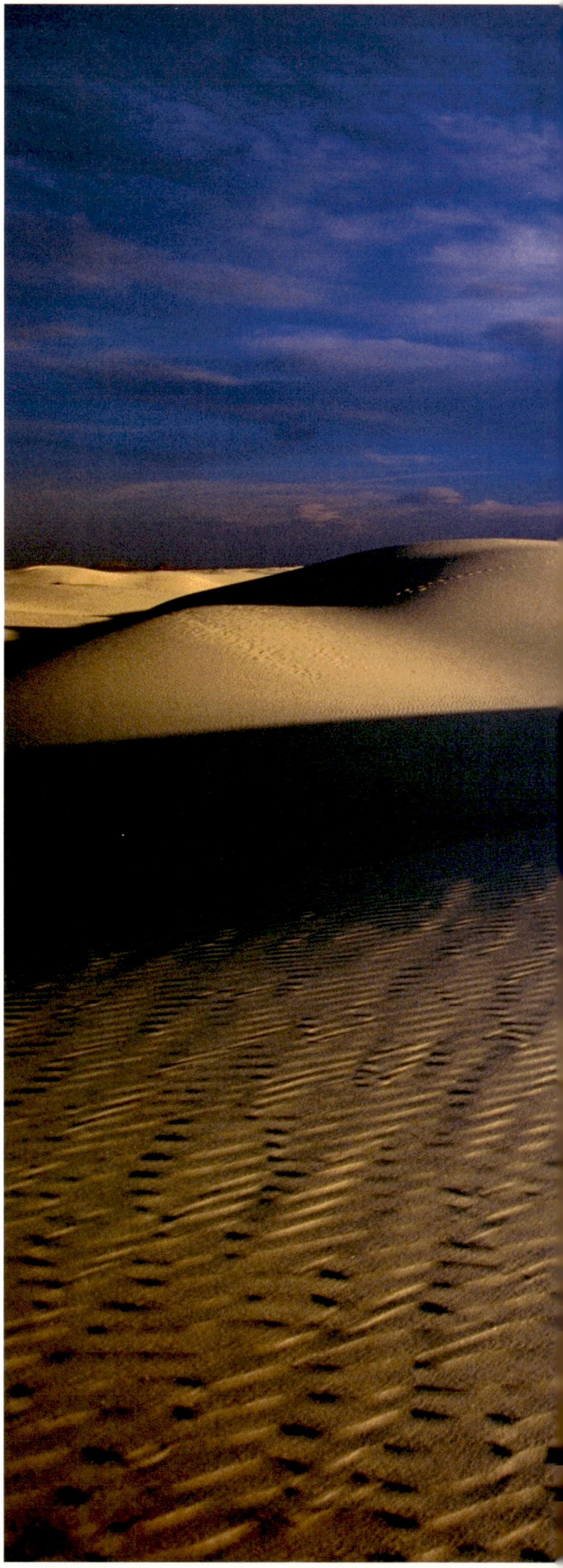

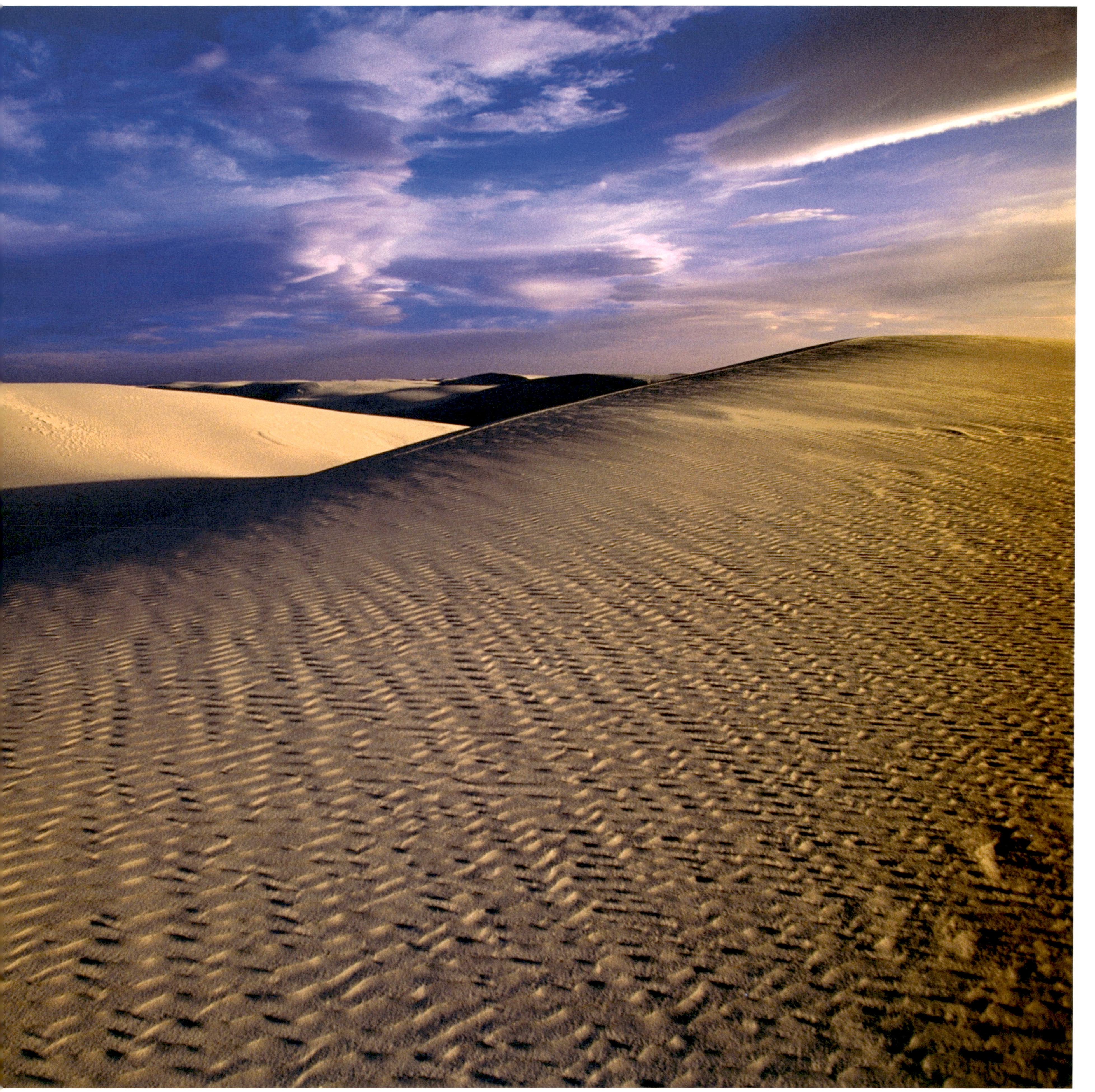

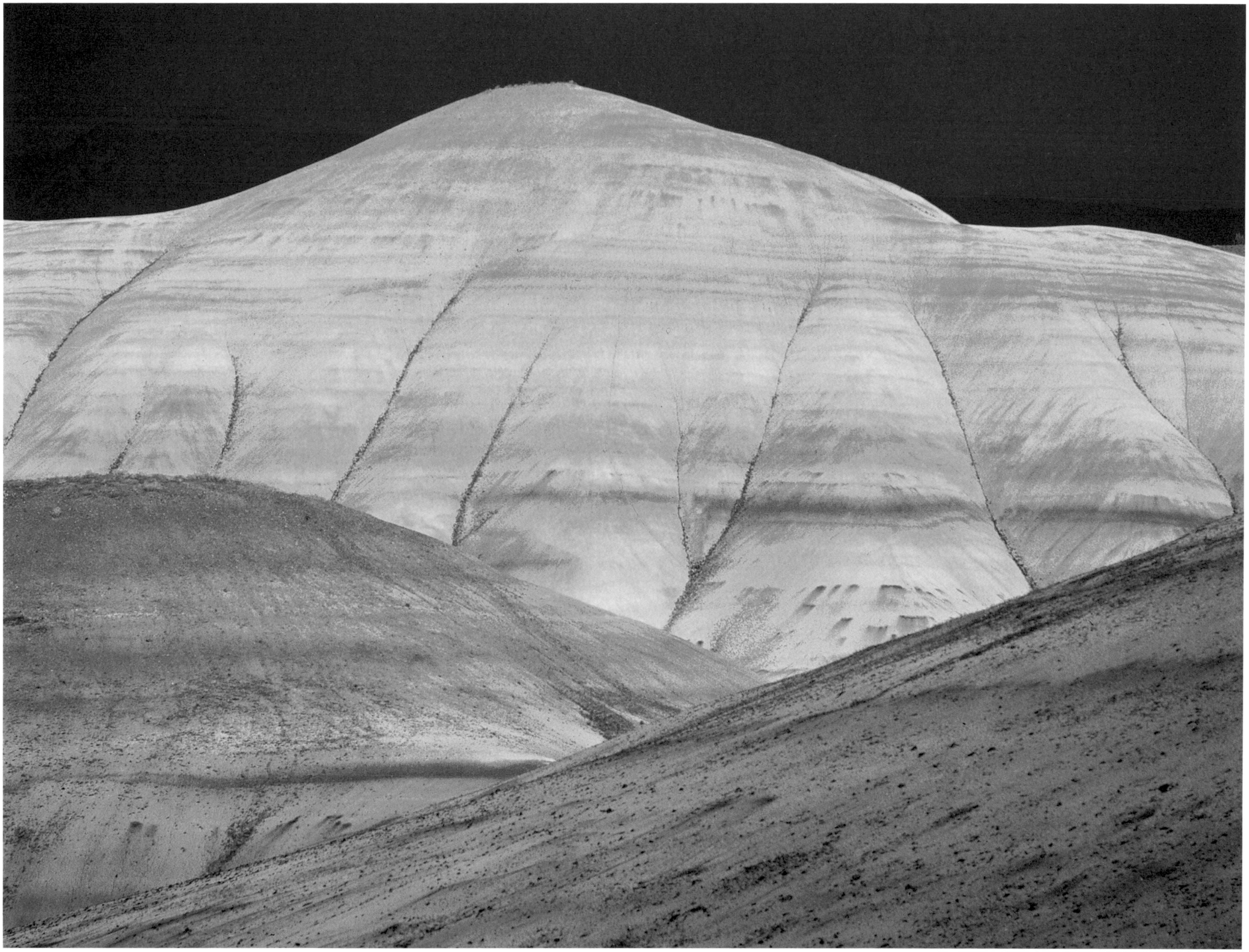

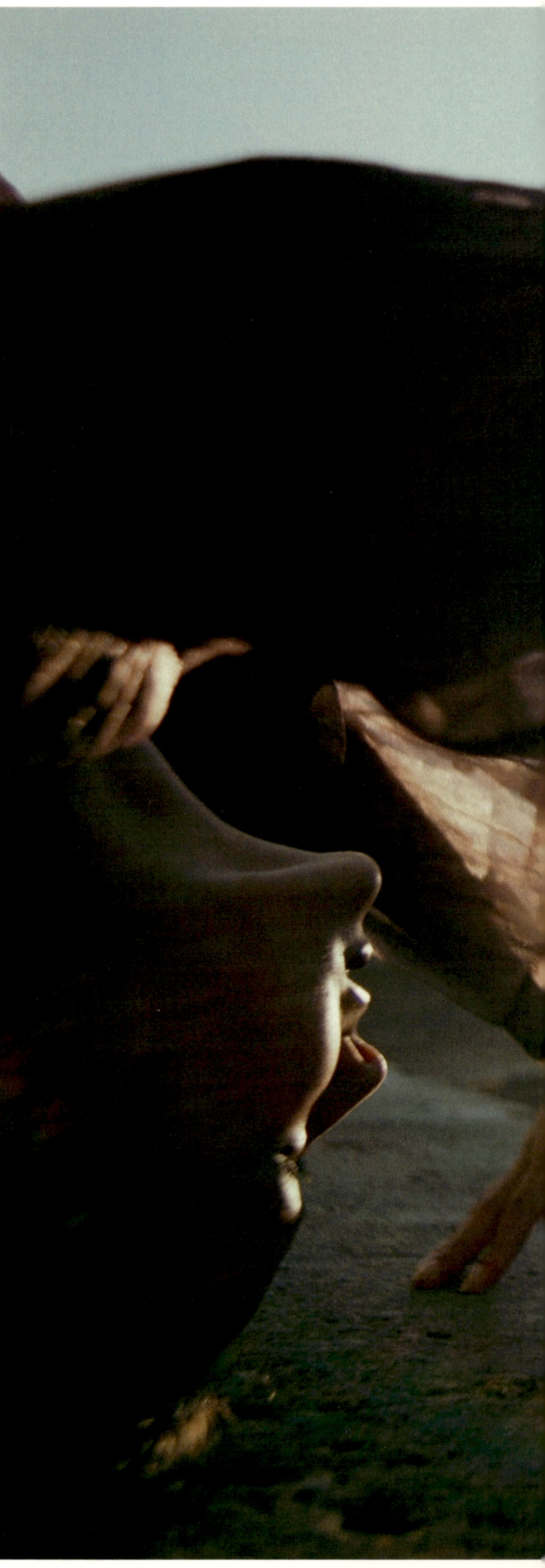

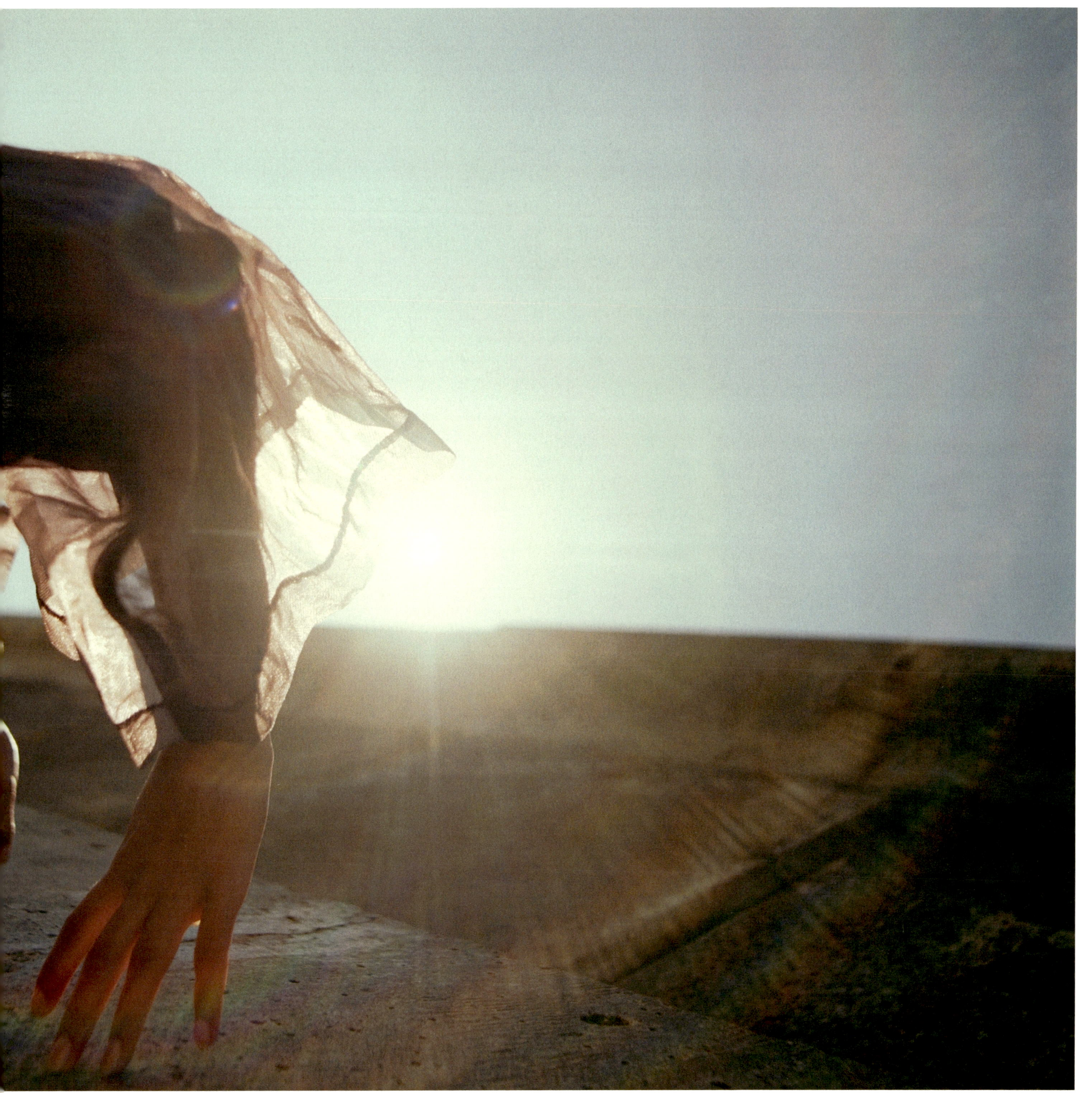

THE MOST PRECIOUS THINGS IN LIFE
ARE THOSE WHICH MONEY CANNOT BUY.

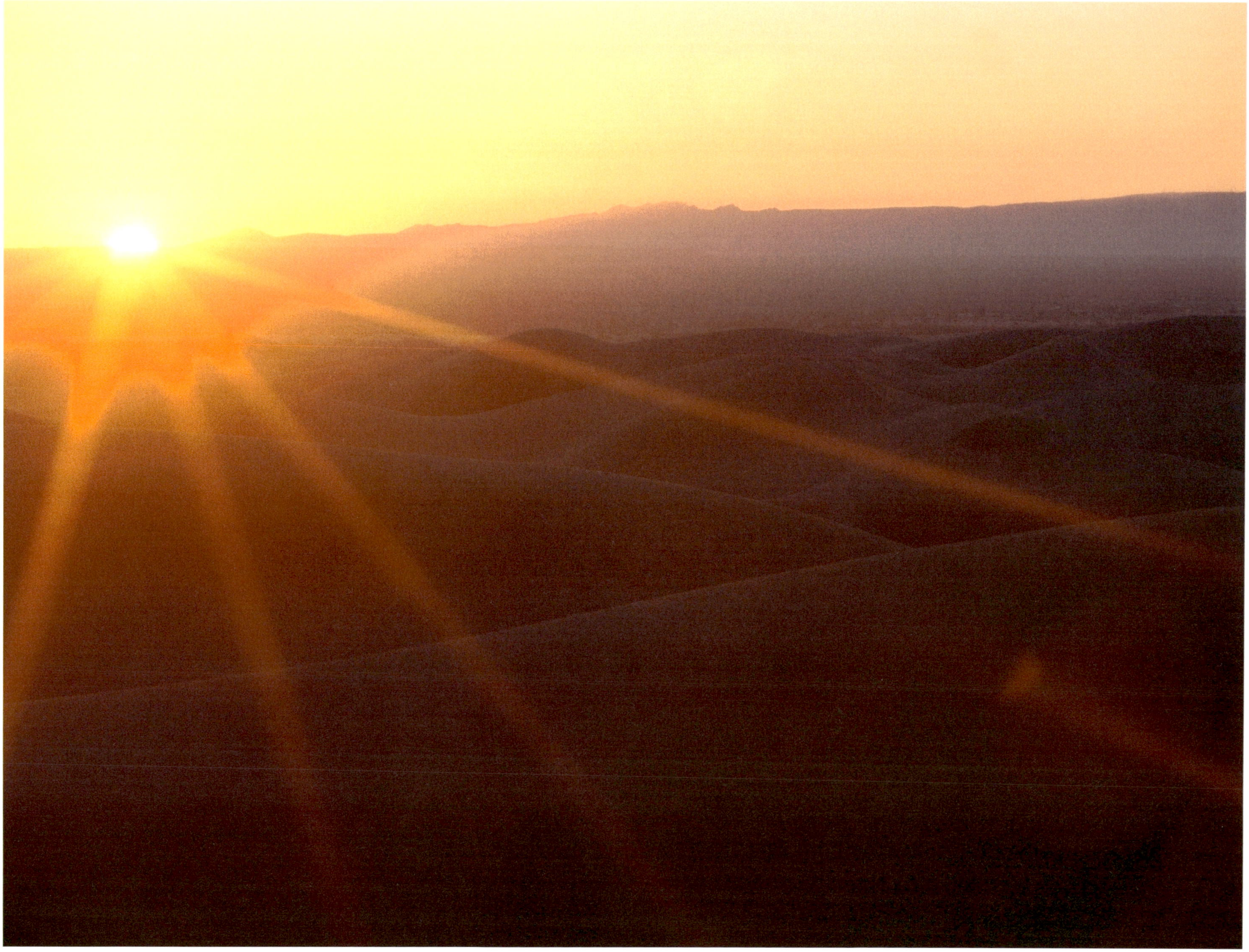

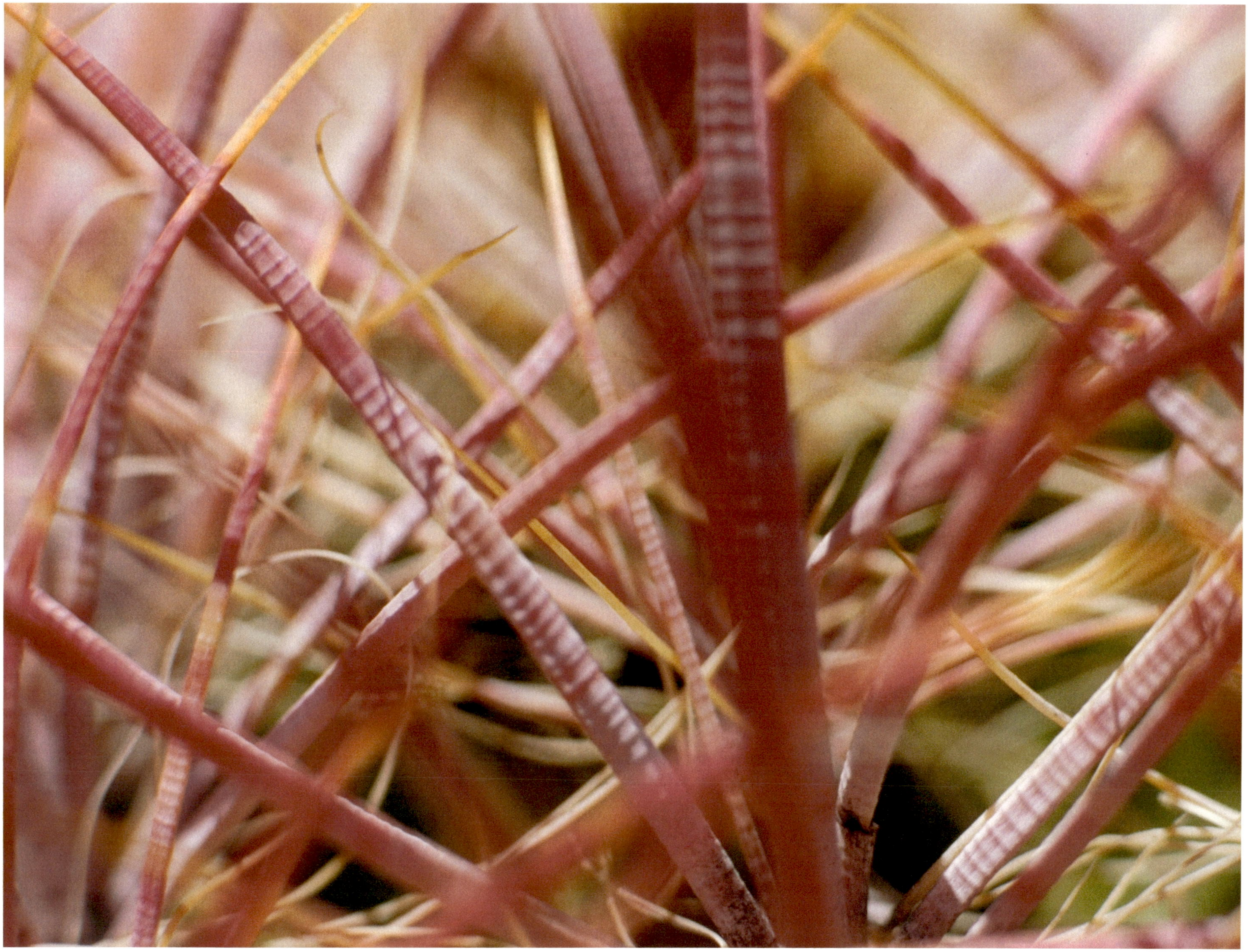

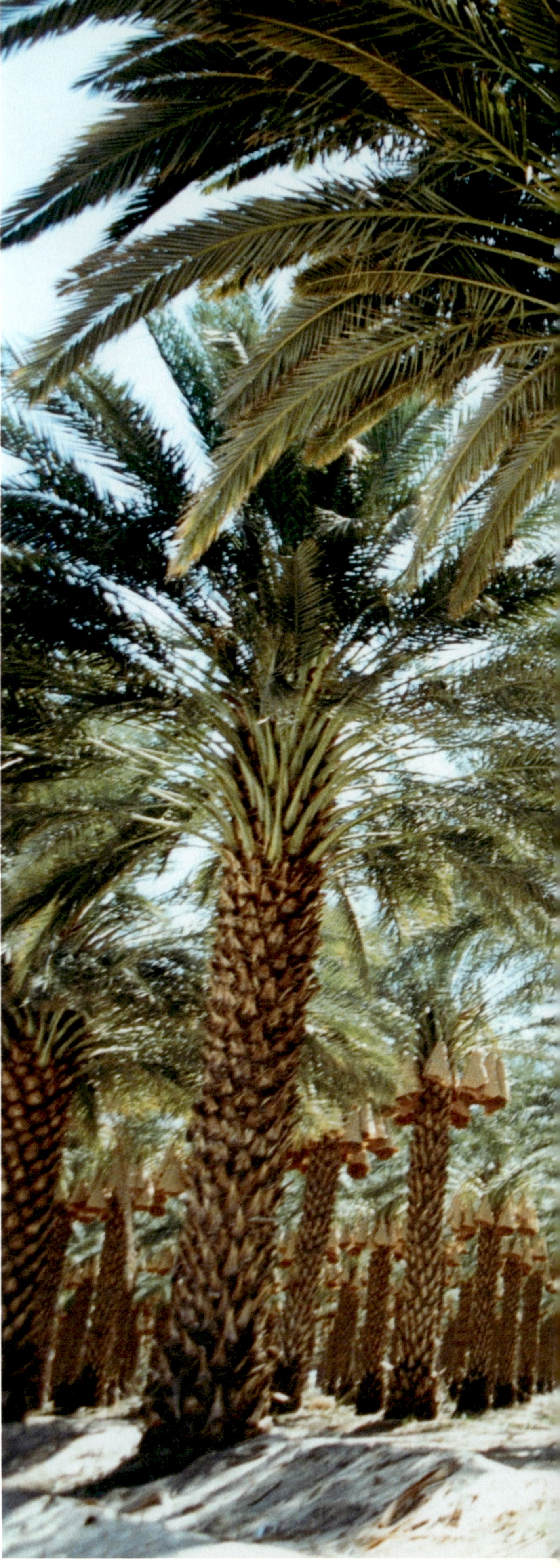

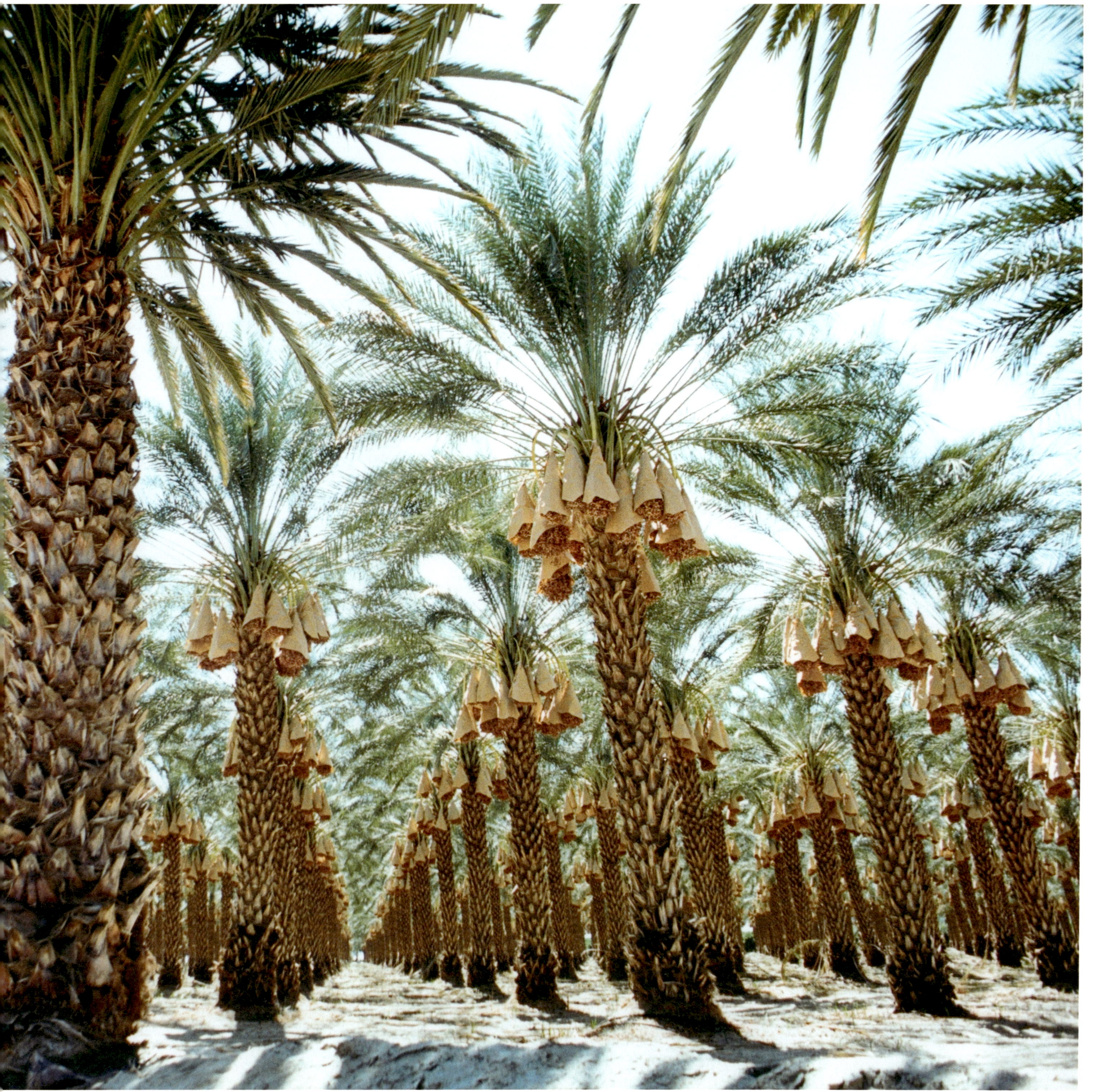

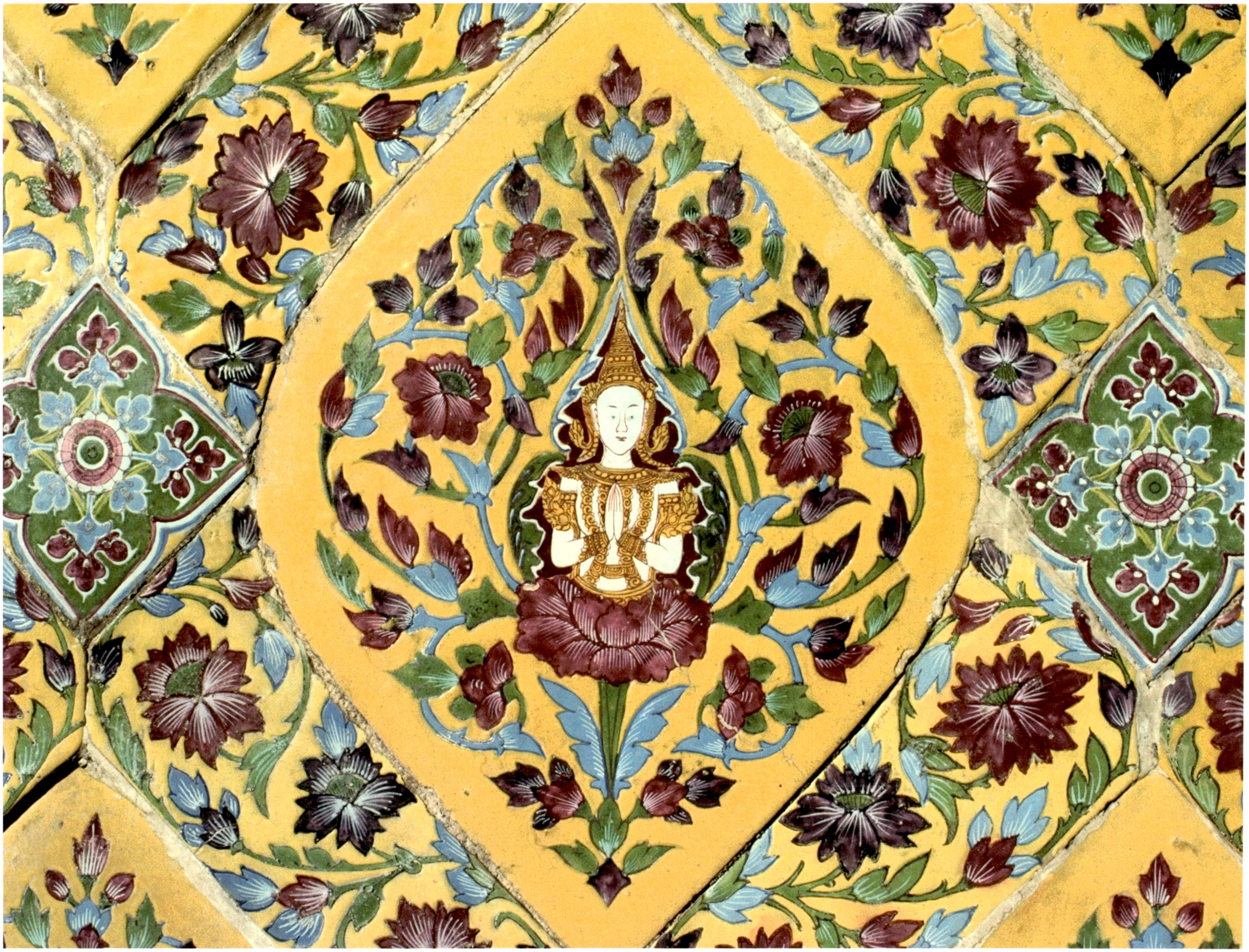

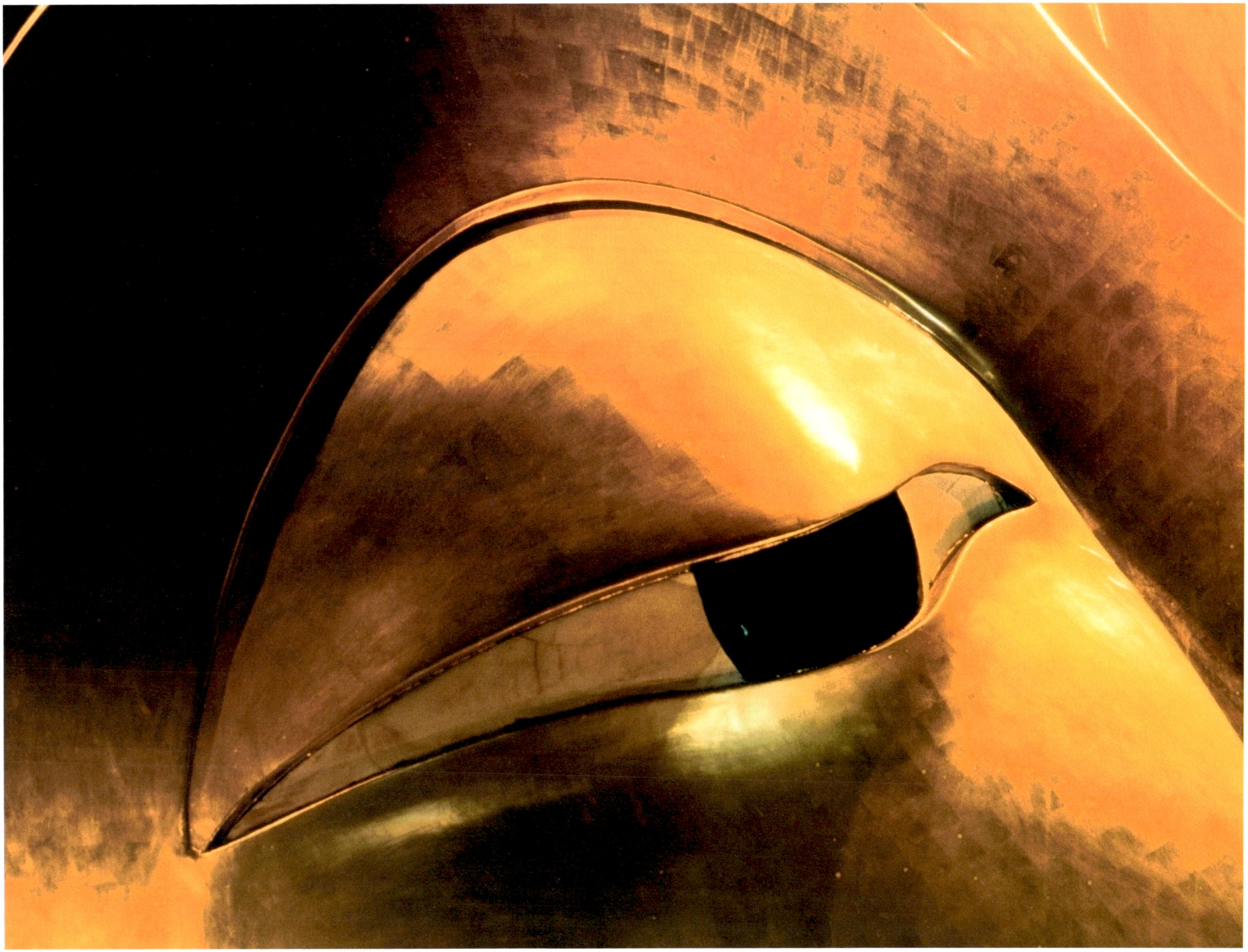

I GO INSIDE MYSELF IN ORDER TO EMERGE.

ANAIS NIN

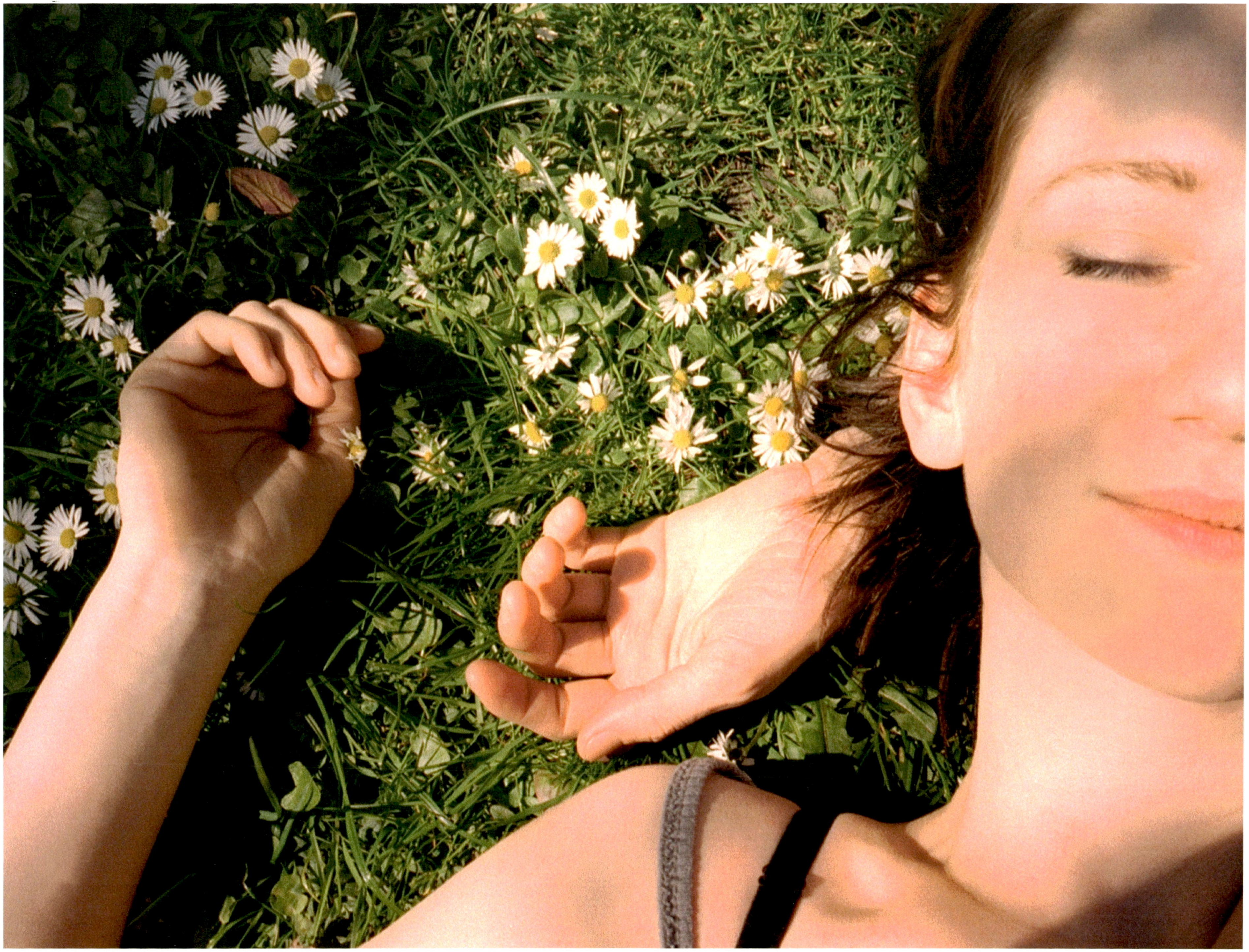

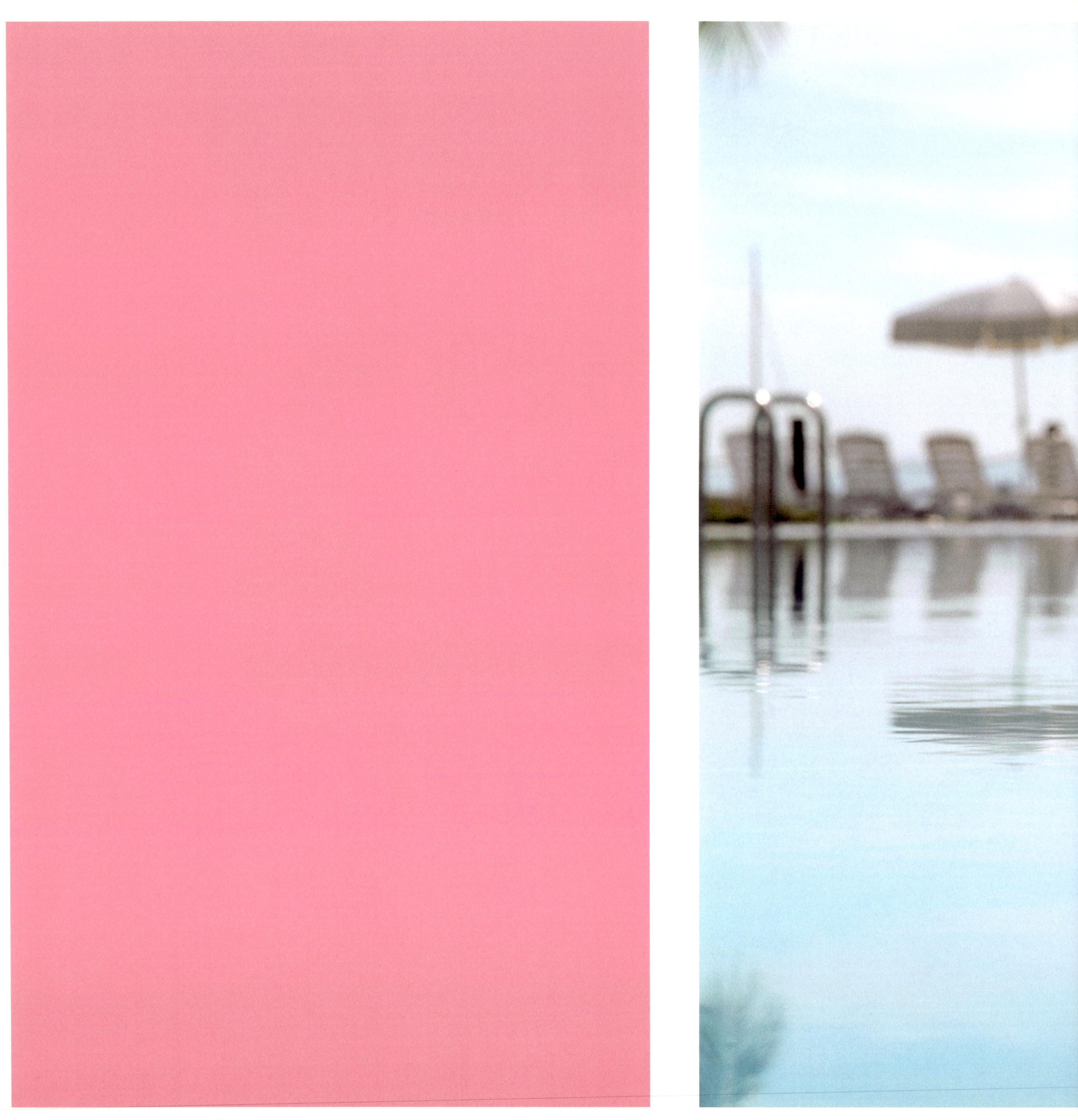

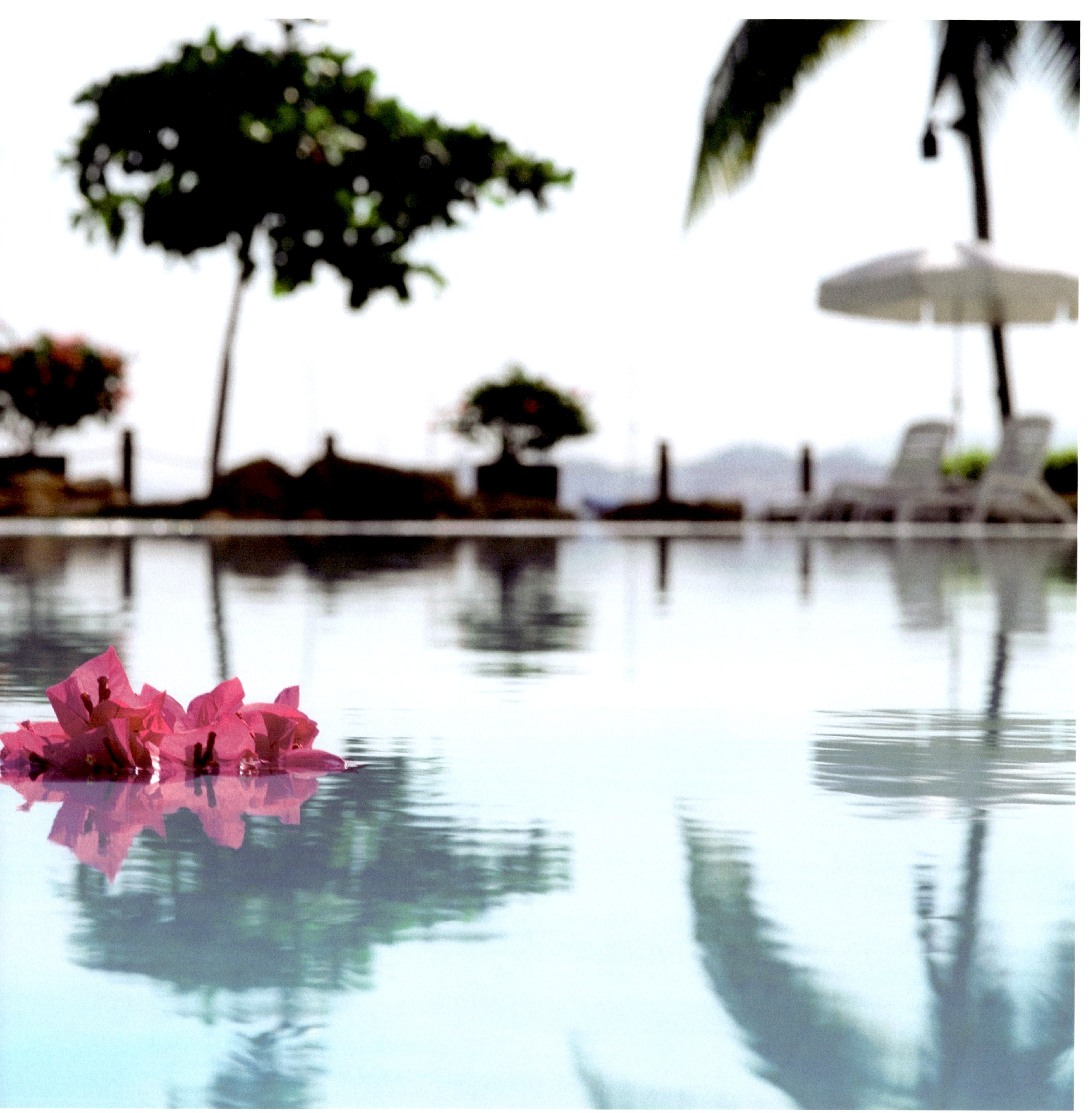

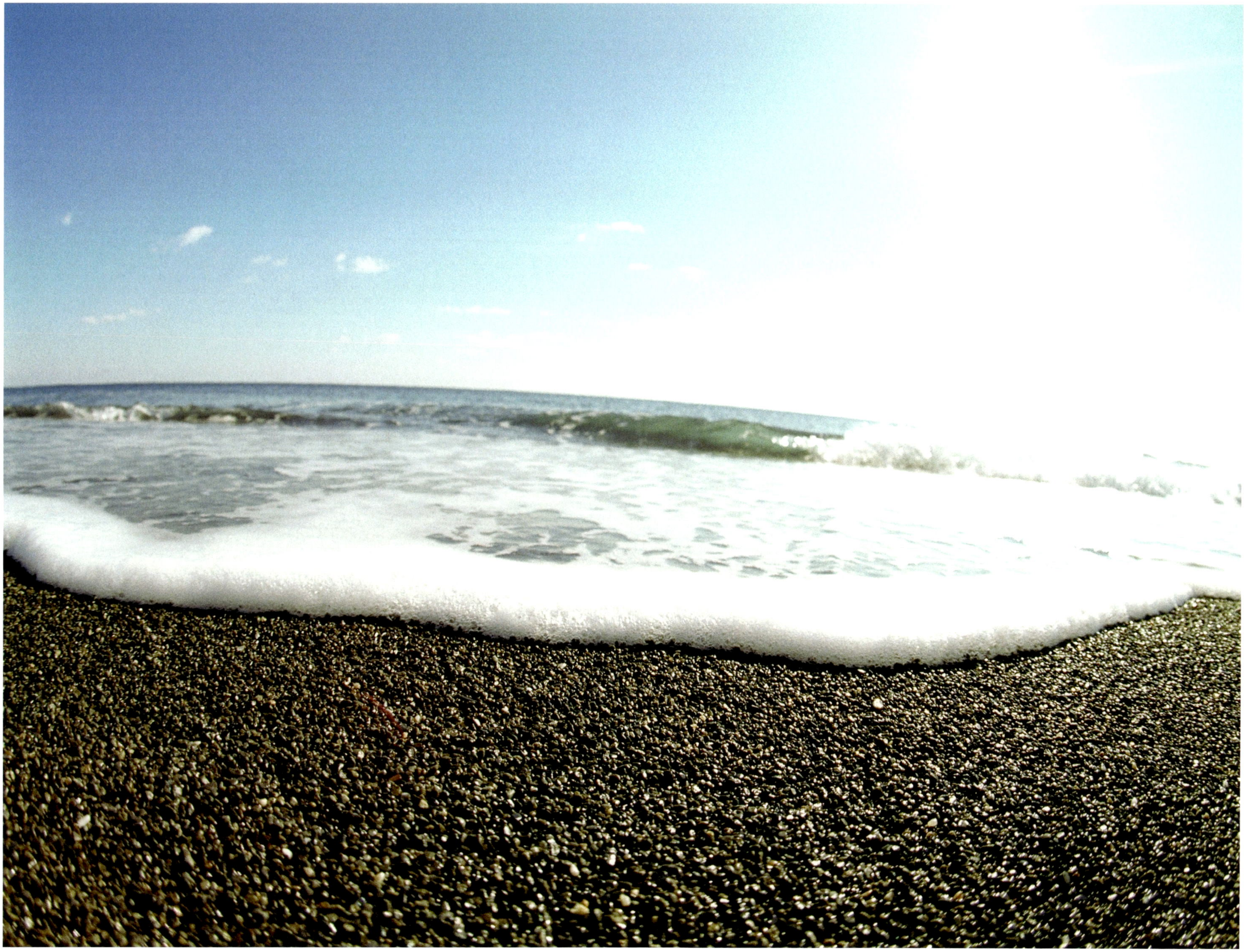

NOTHING IS MORE THERAPEUTIC FOR THE SOUL
THAN THE SENSES, JUST AS ONLY THE SOUL CAN
HEAL THE SENSES.

OSCAR WILDE

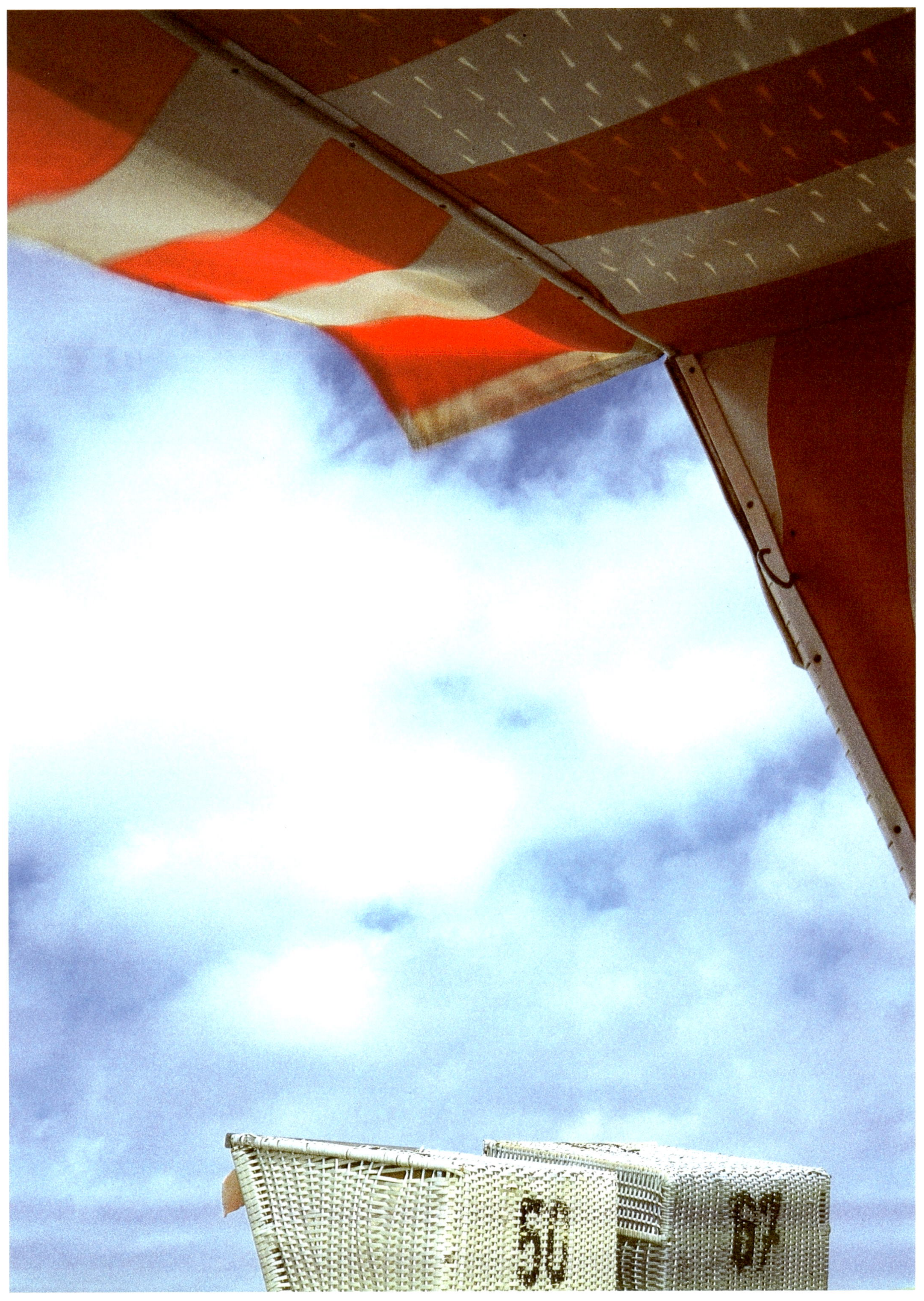

80

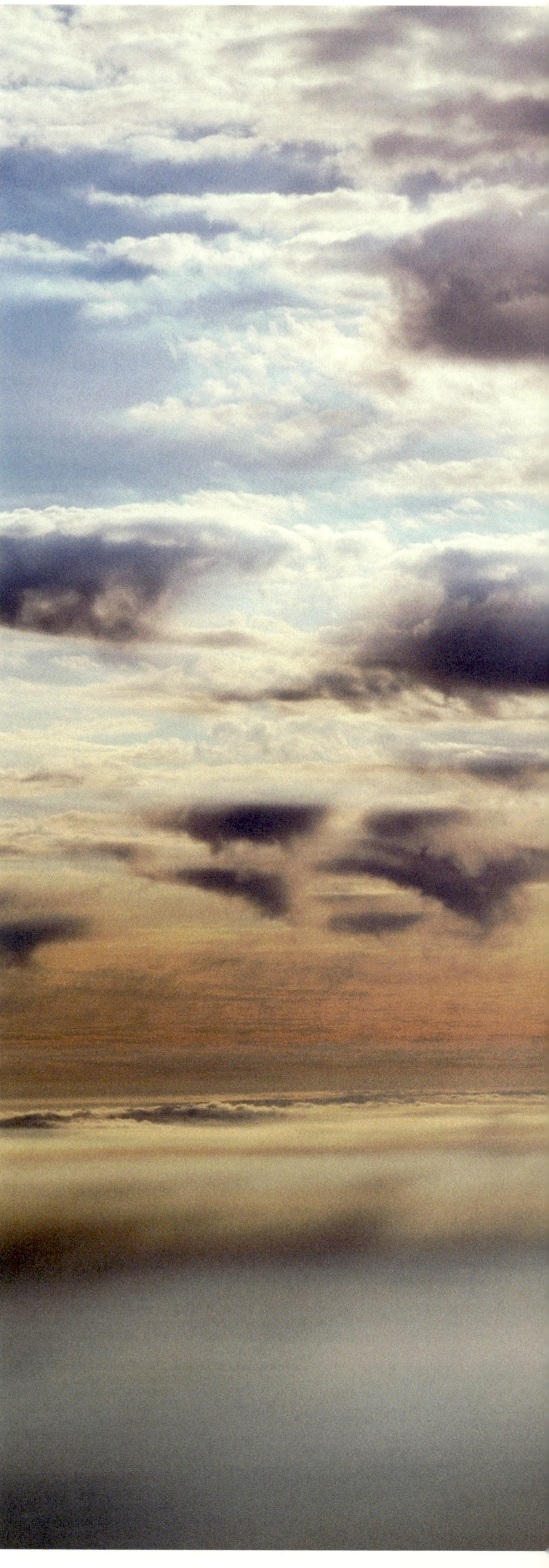

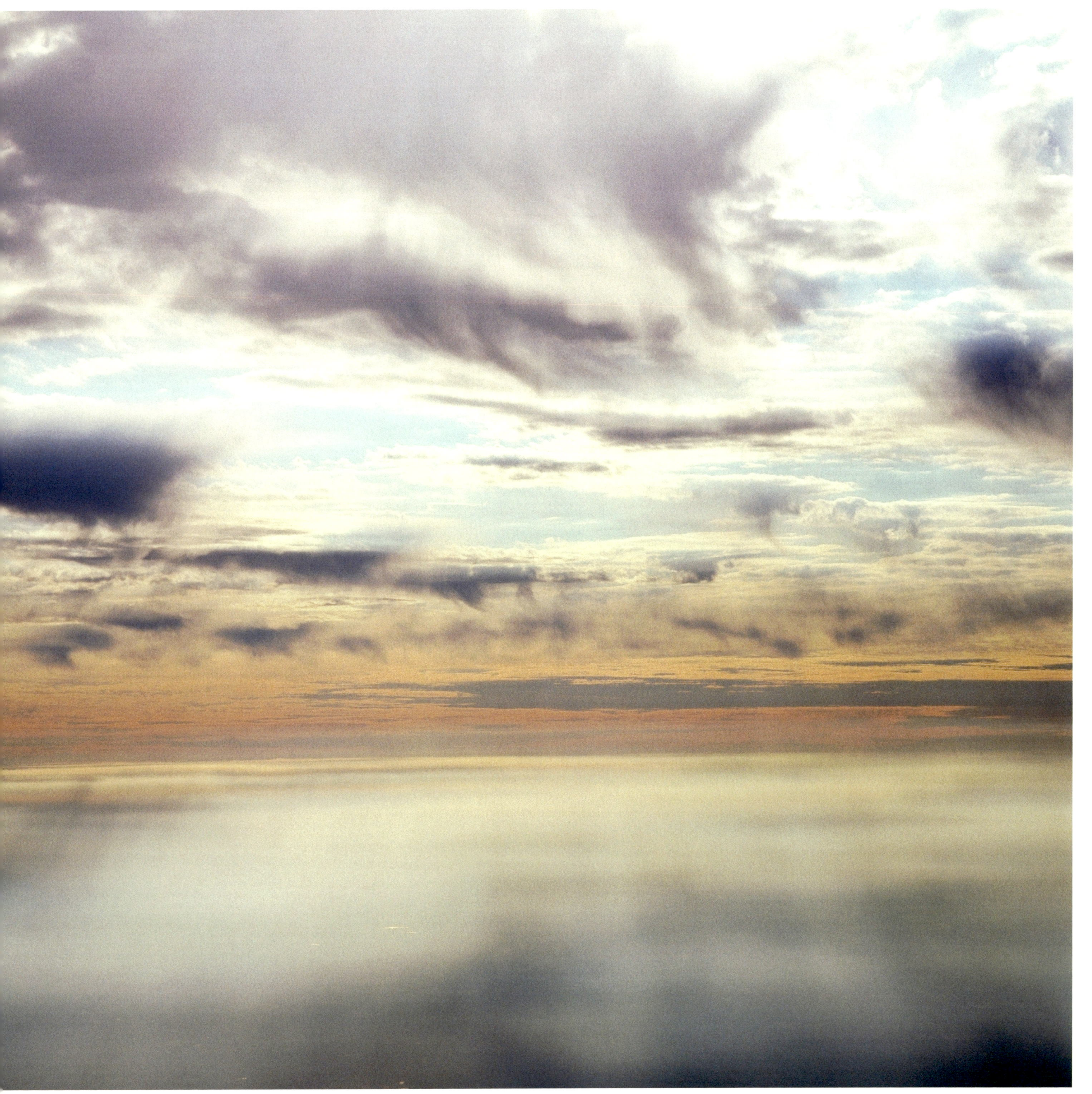

THE GREATEST REVELATION IS PEACE.

LAO-TSE

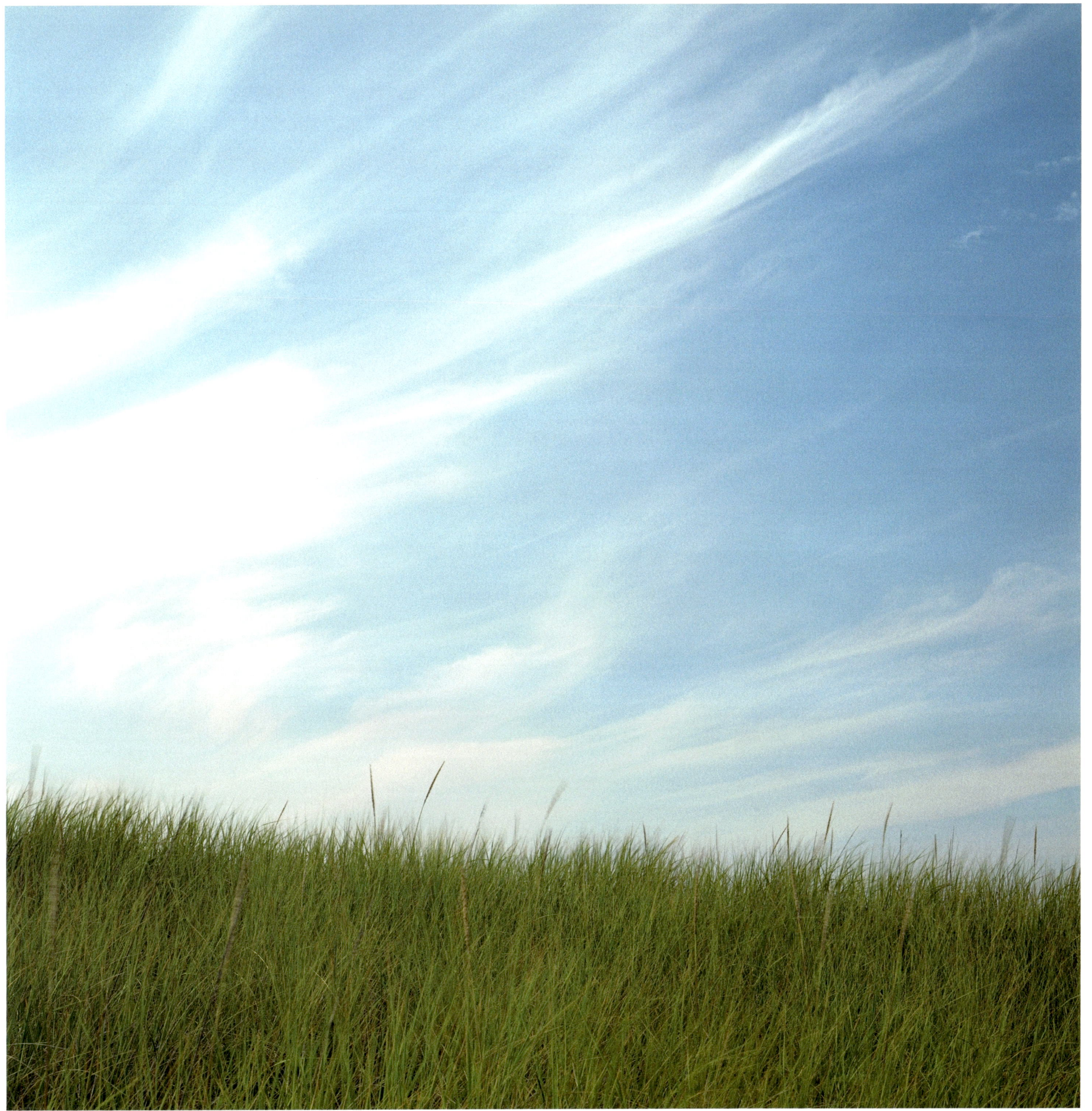

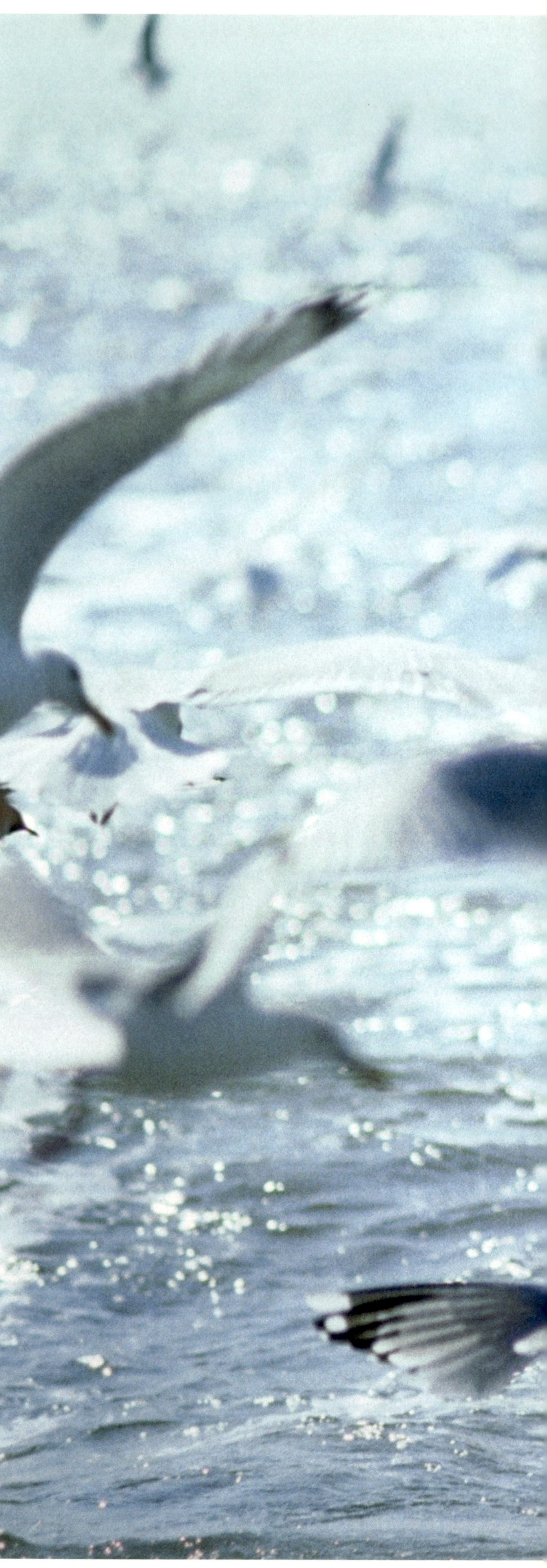

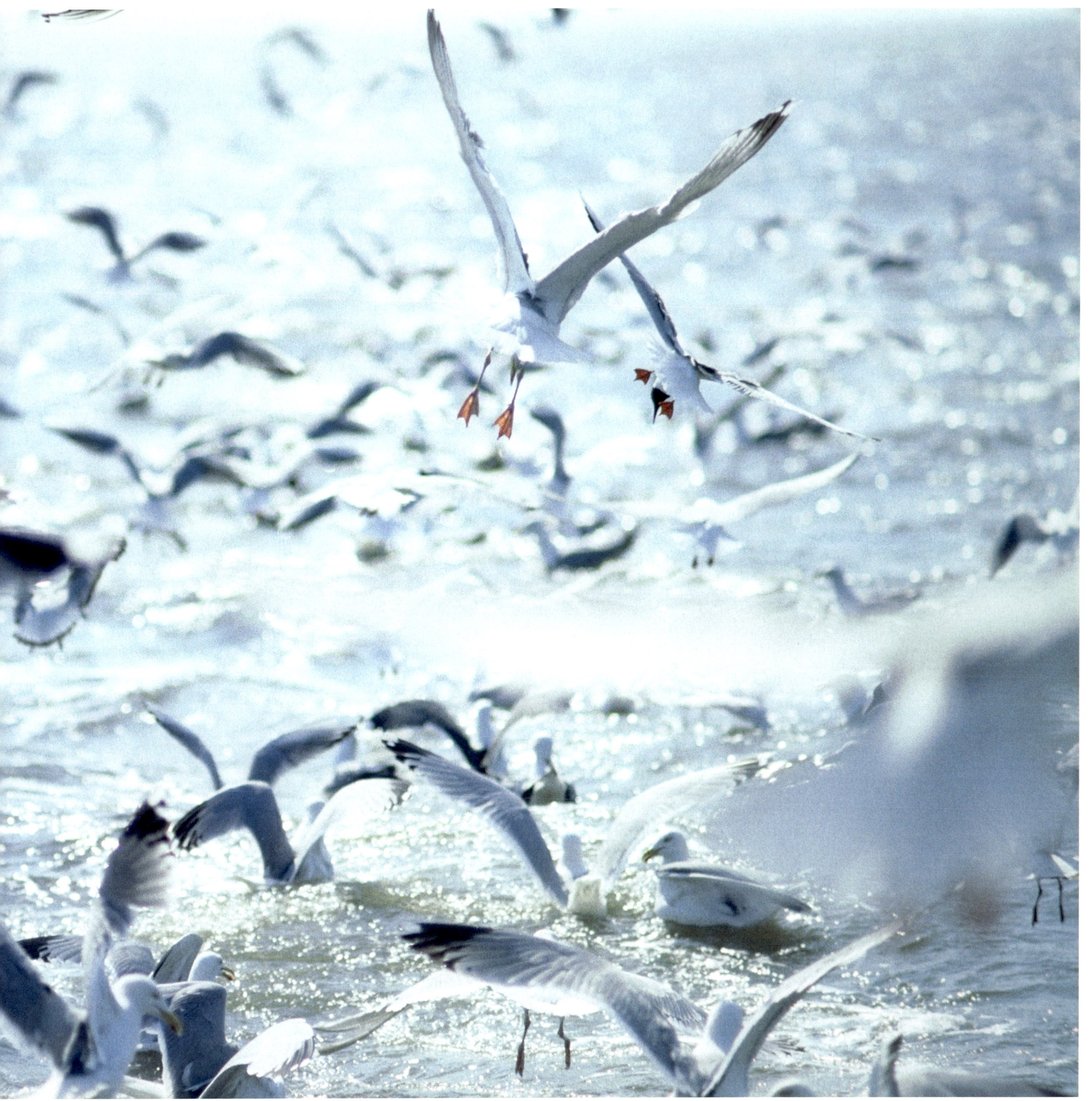

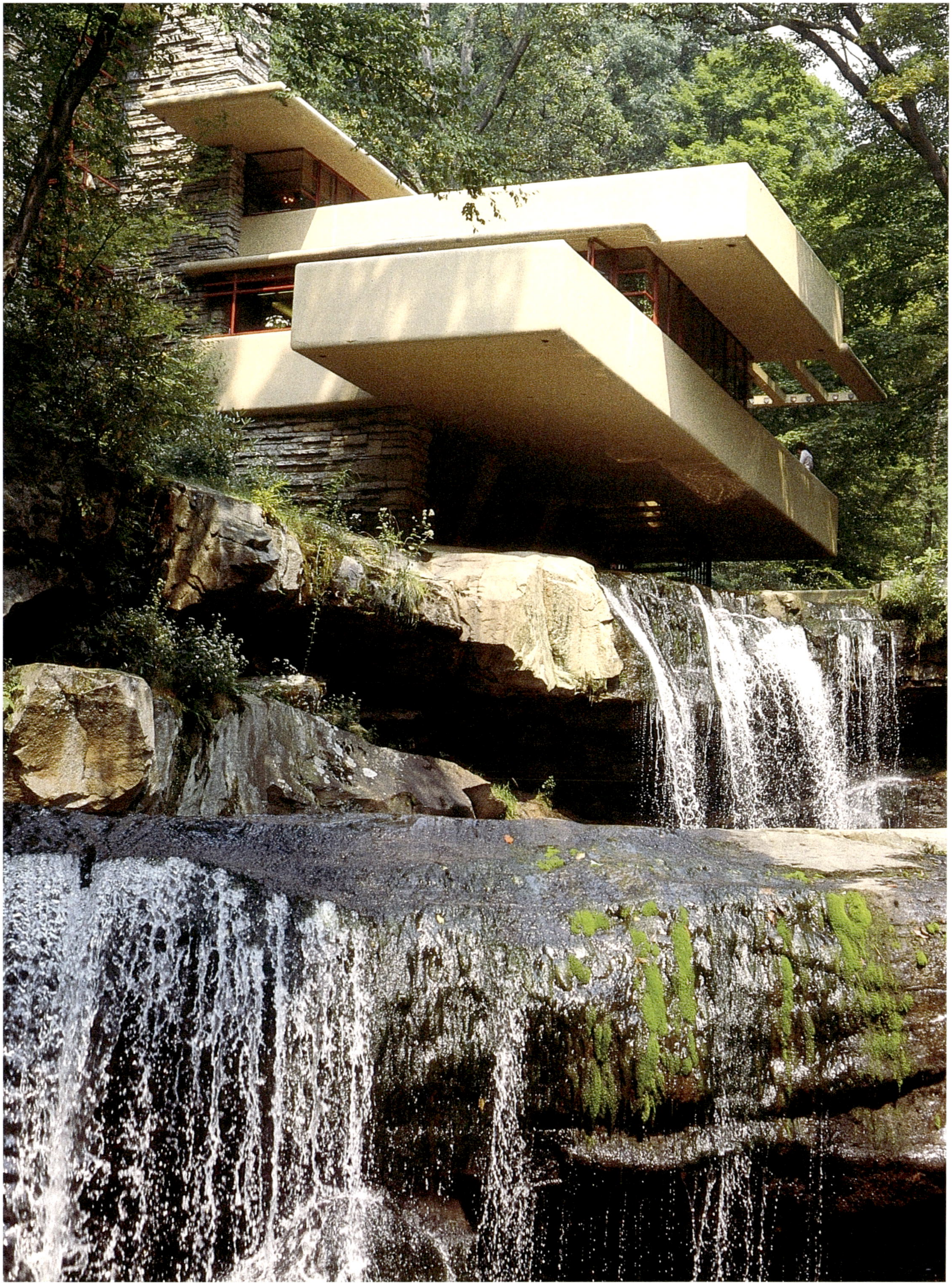

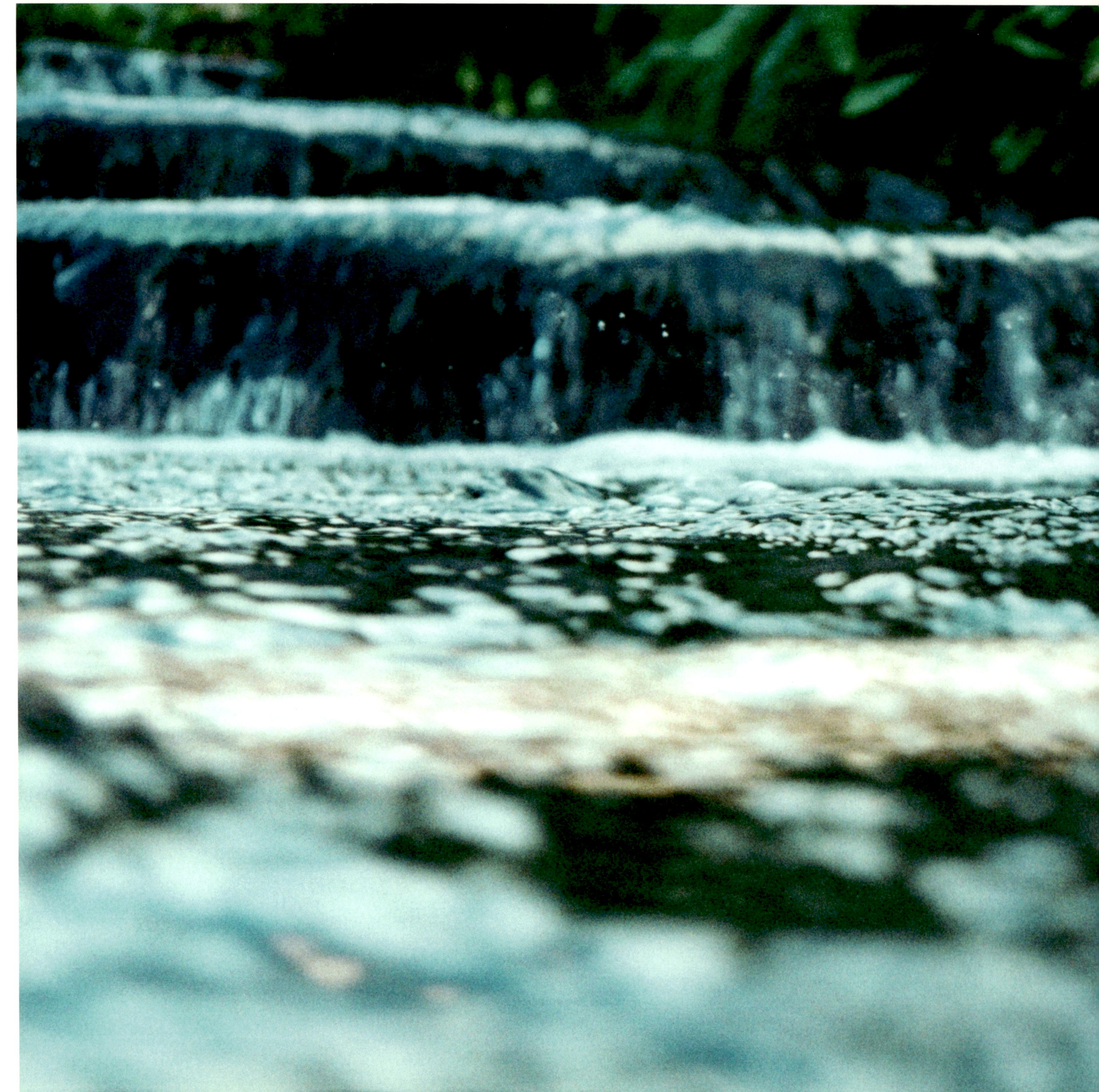

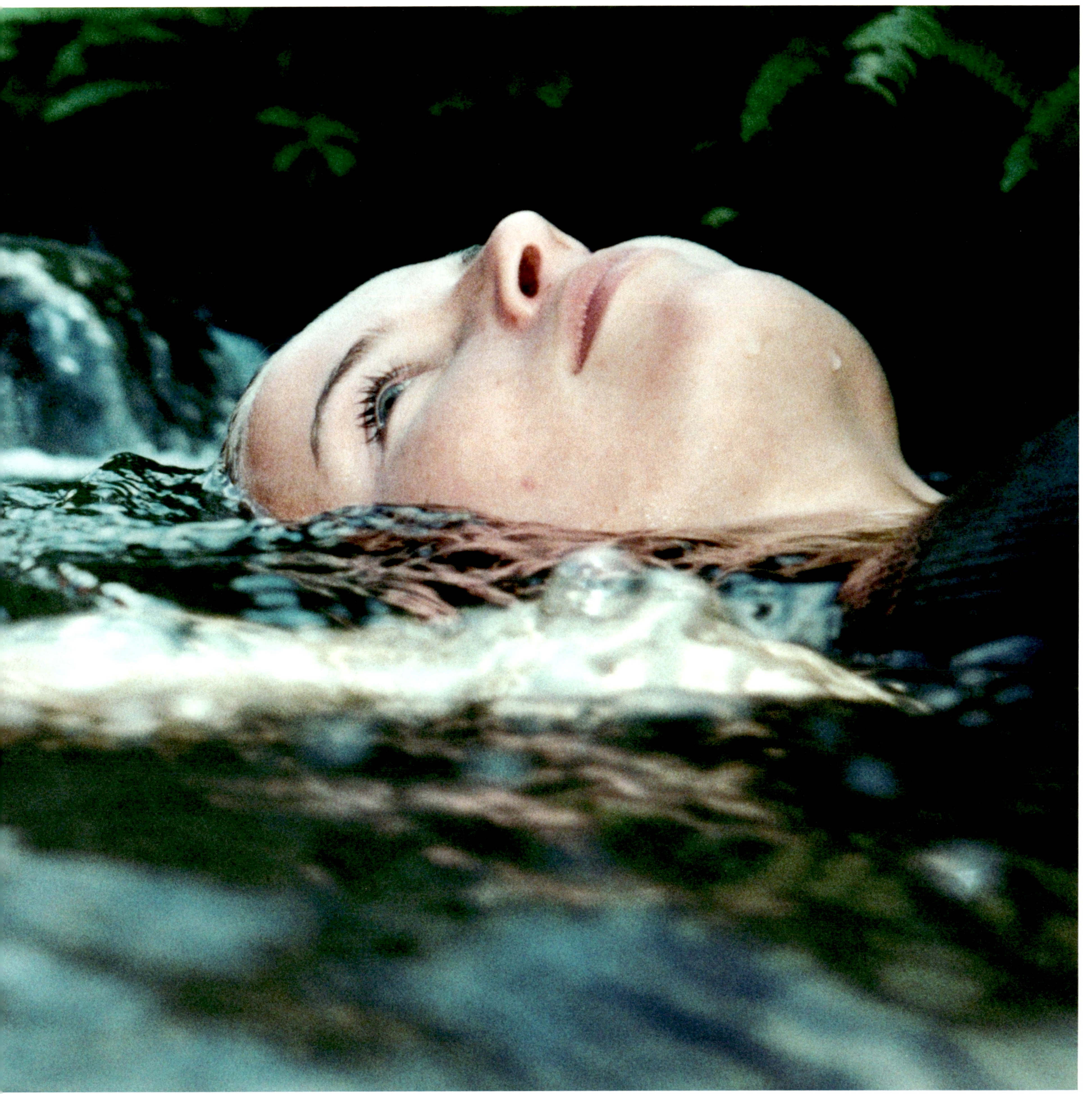

IN ORDER TO SEE NEW PERSPECTIVES IT IS
OFTEN ENOUGH TO LOOK AT THINGS FROM A
DIFFERENT ANGLE.

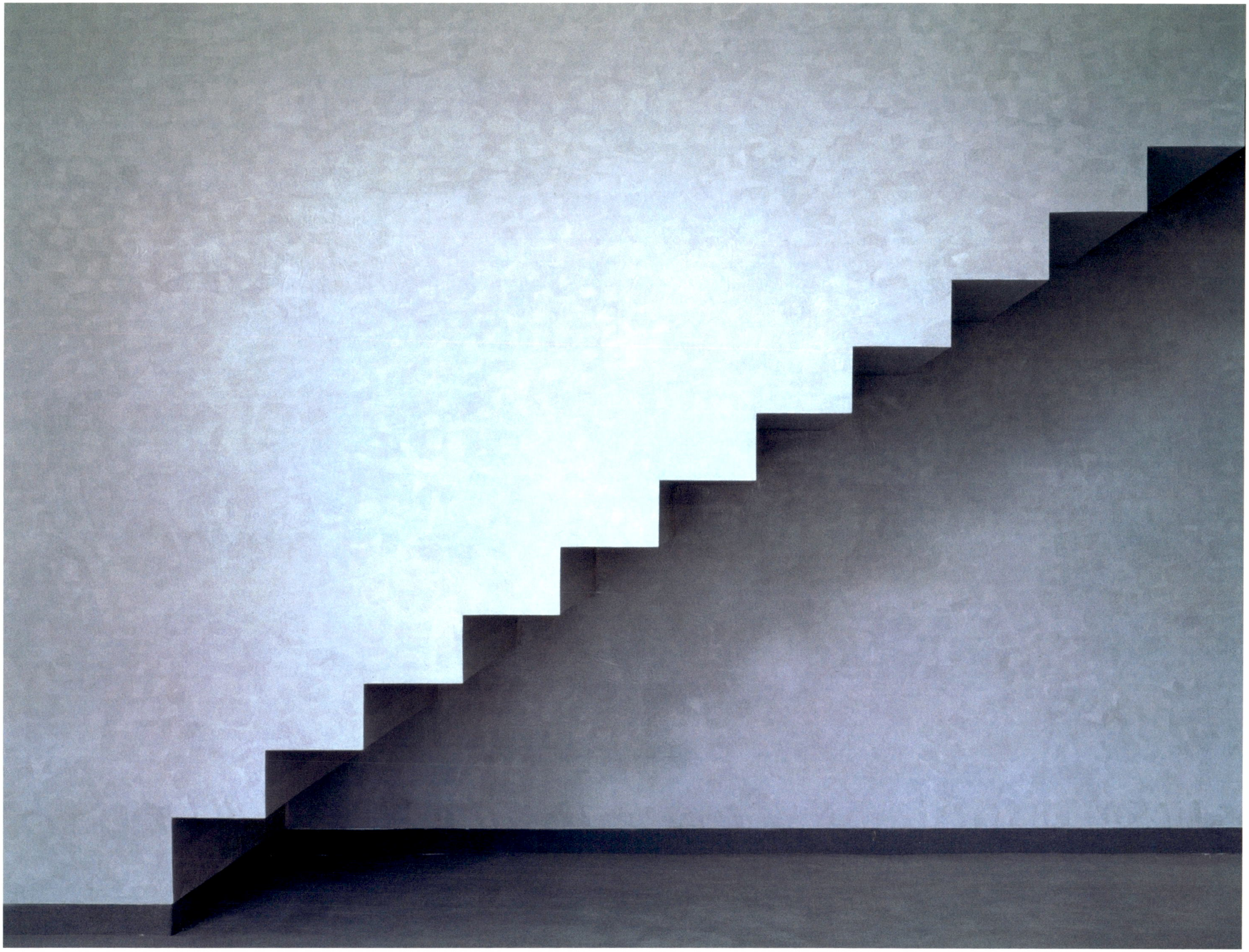

SUBMERGE (VERB).
1. TO GO UNDER WATER, DISAPPEAR
(FOR A SHORT OR LONGER
PERIOD OF TIME) UNDER WATER.
2. (FIGURATIVE USE) TO FEEL
WELL, TO IMMERSE ONESELF IN
ANOTHER WORLD

WAHRIG'S DICTIONARY DEFINITIONS

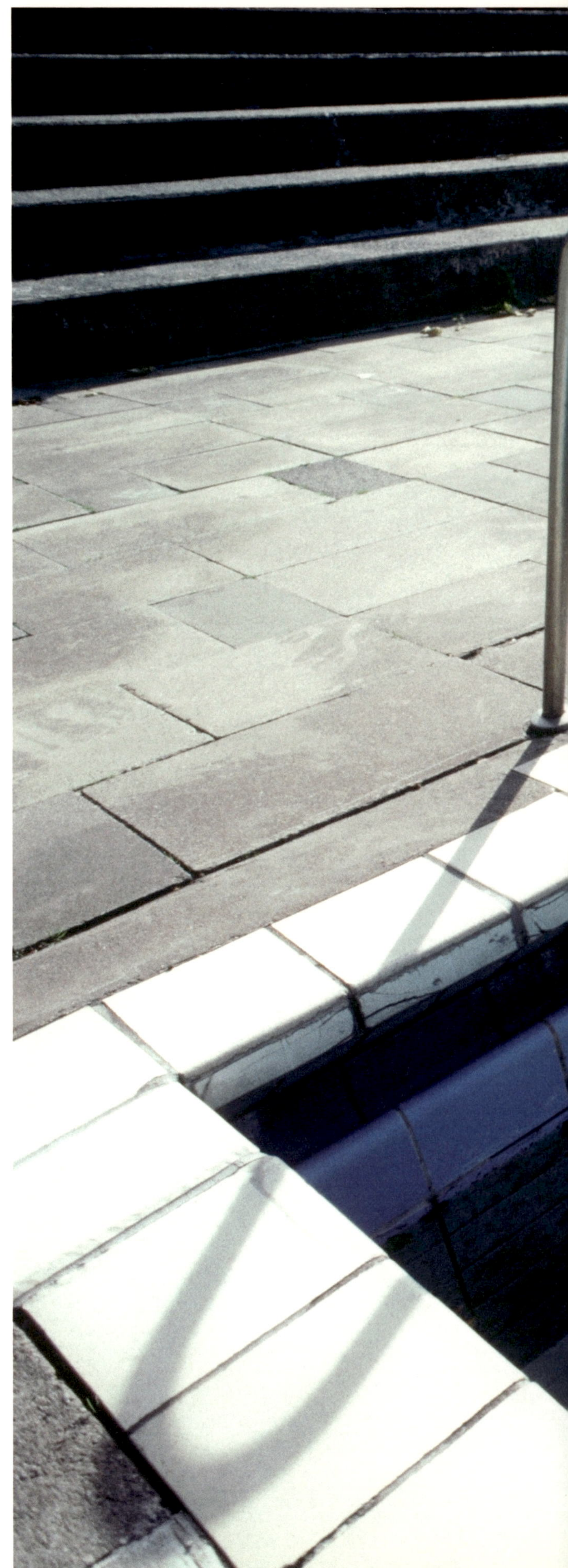

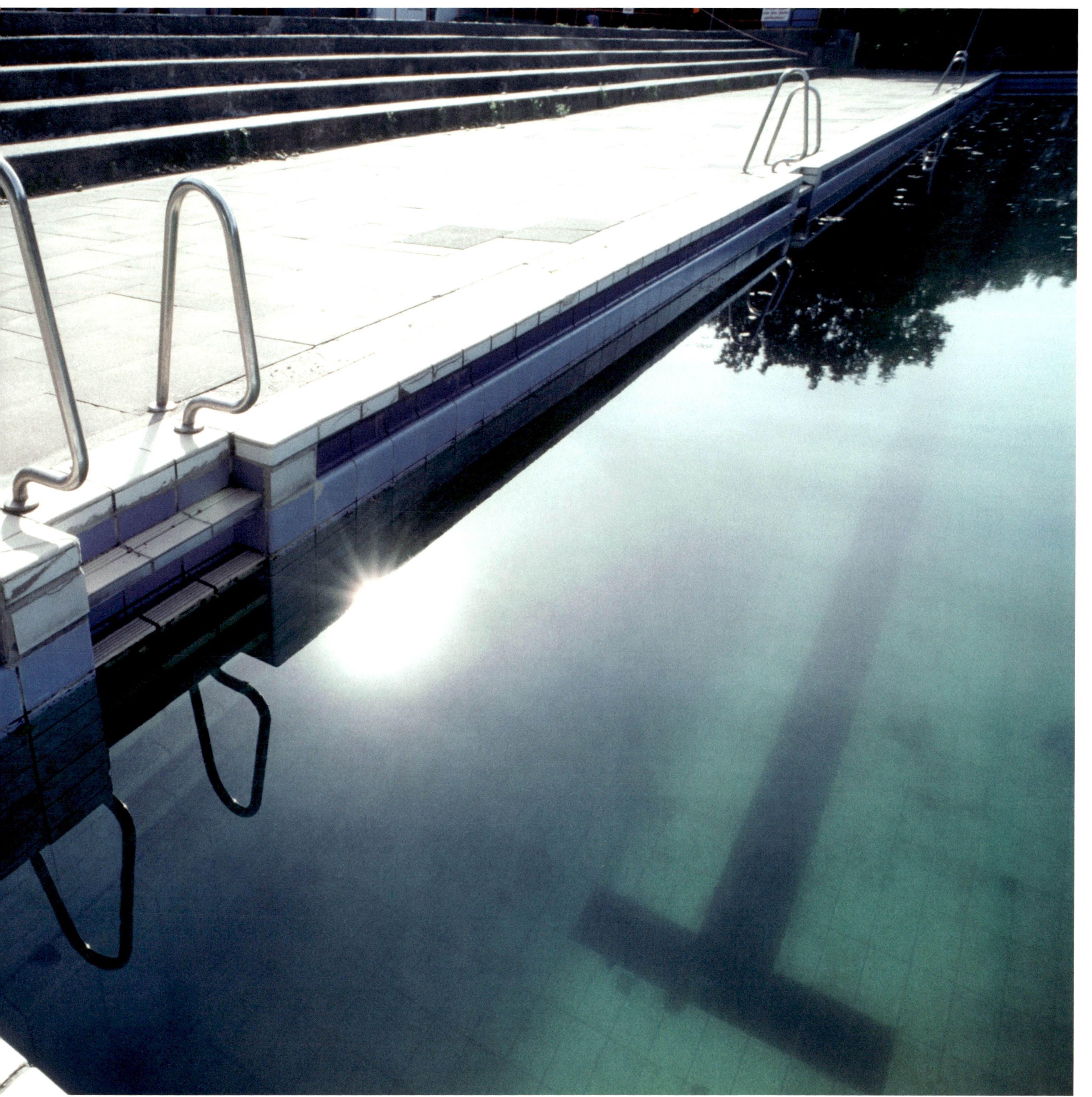

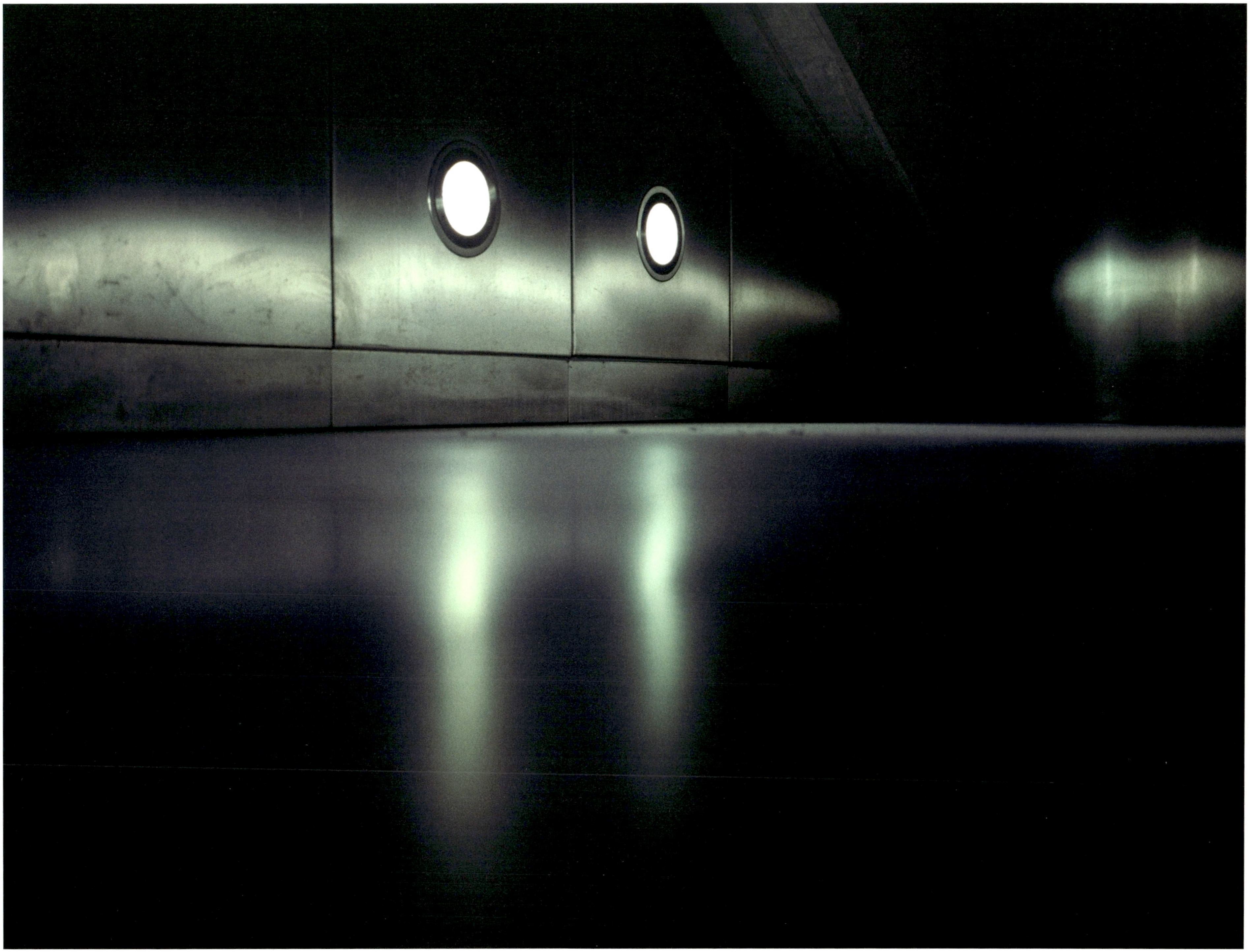

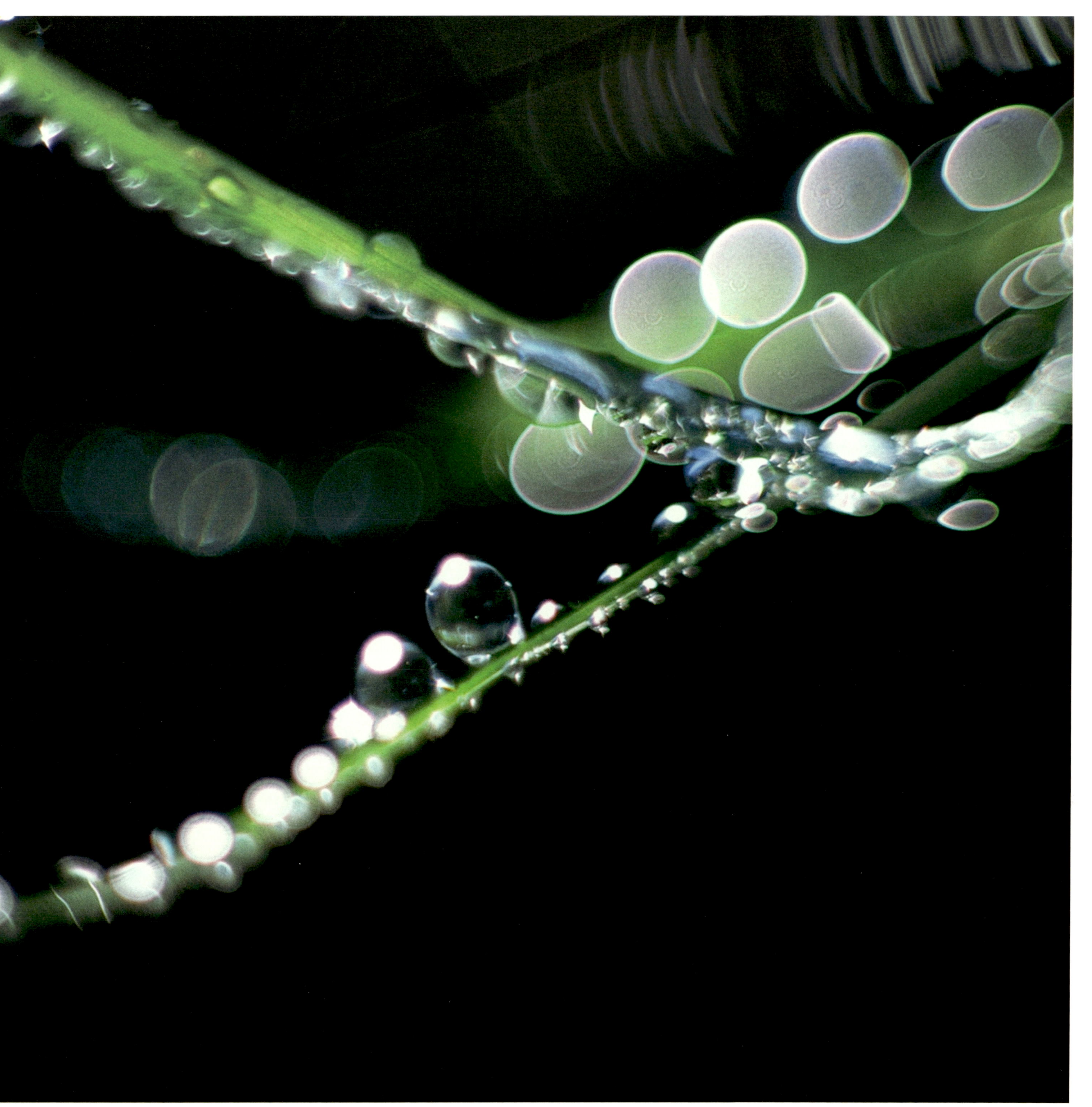

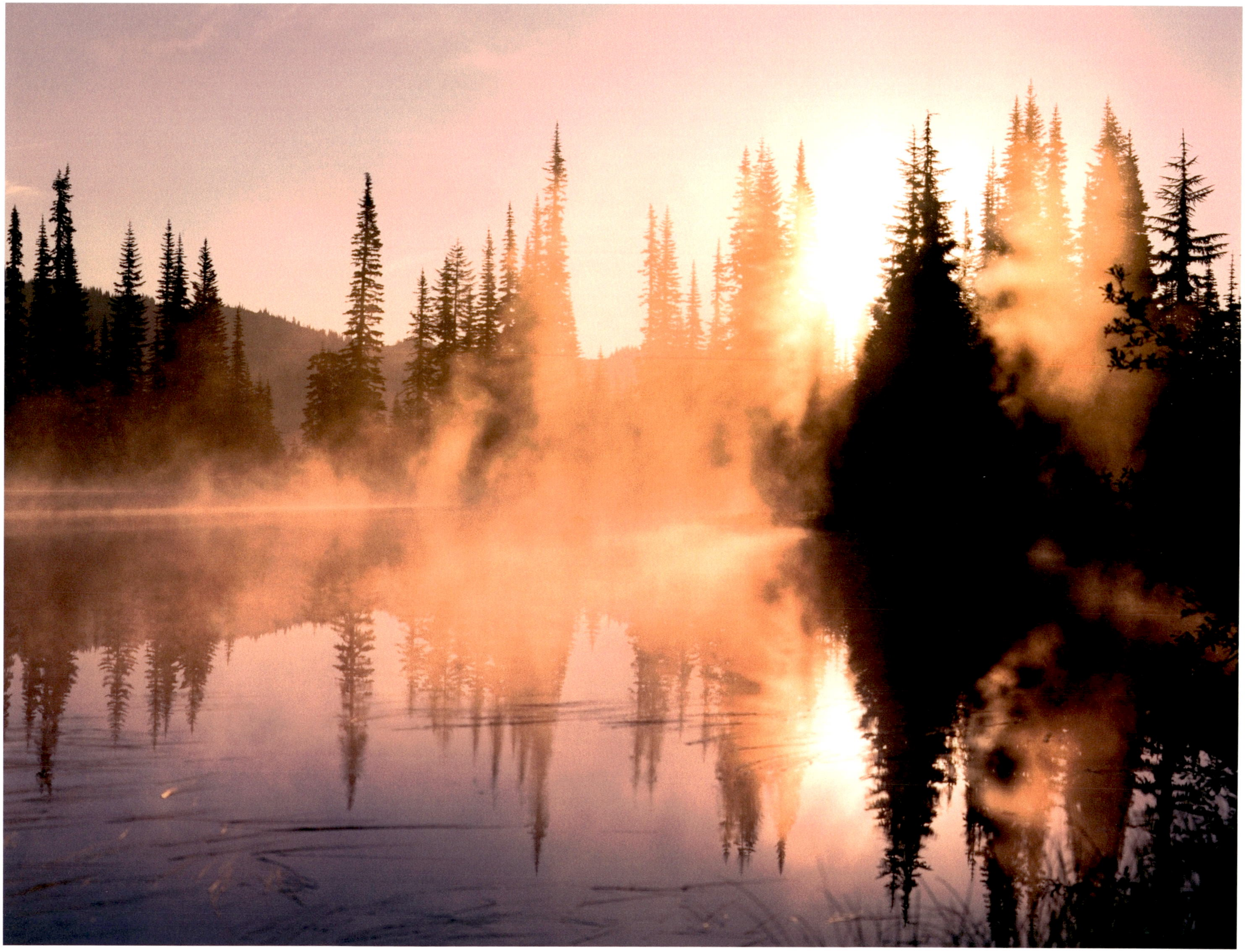

ALL PEOPLE AND THINGS HAVE THEIR SPECIAL PERSPECTIVE.
SOME OF THEM MUST BE VIEWED CLOSE UP IN
ORDER TO JUDGE THEM, OTHERS FROM A DISTANCE.

FRANCOIS DE LA ROCHEFOUCAULD

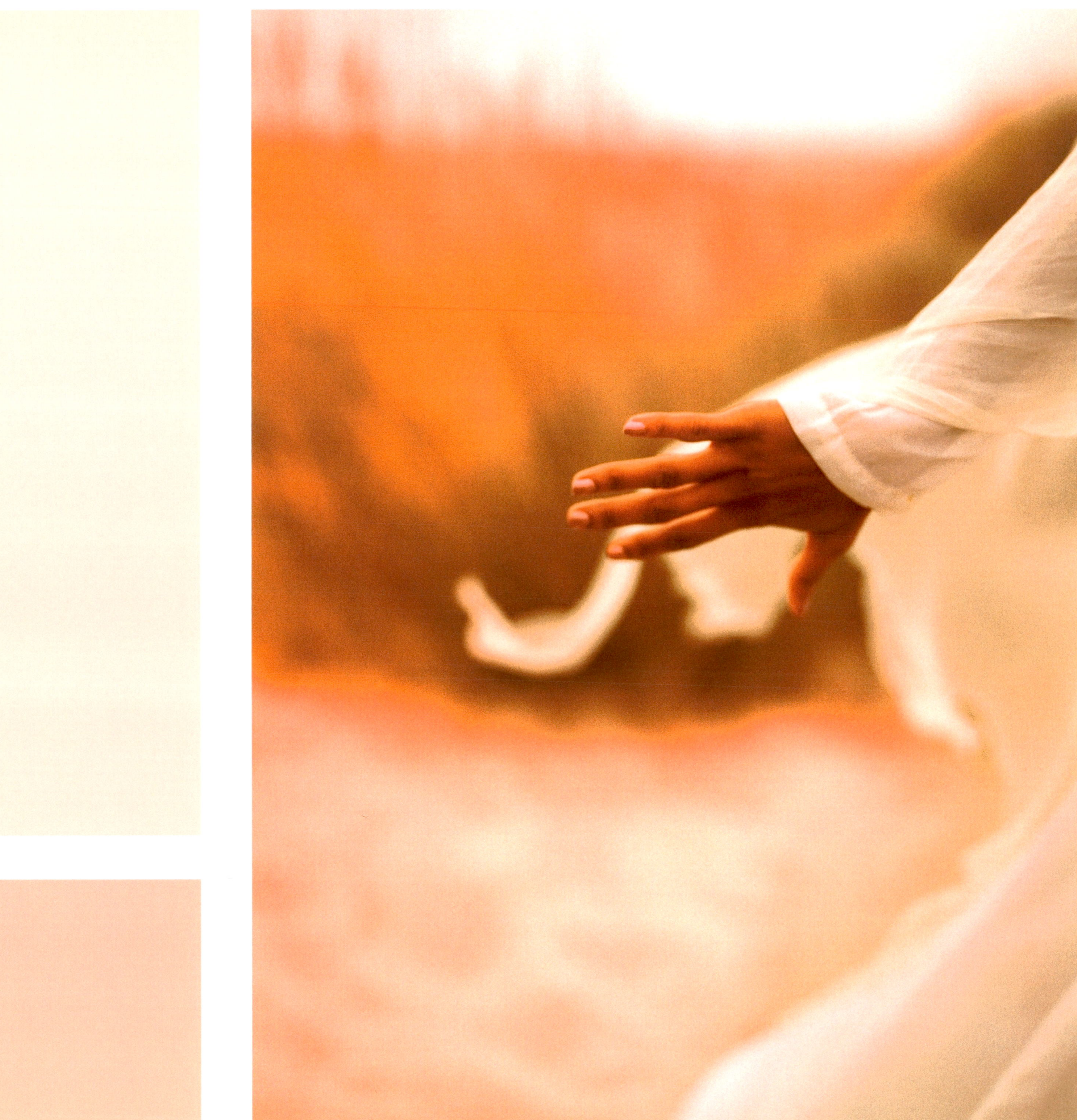

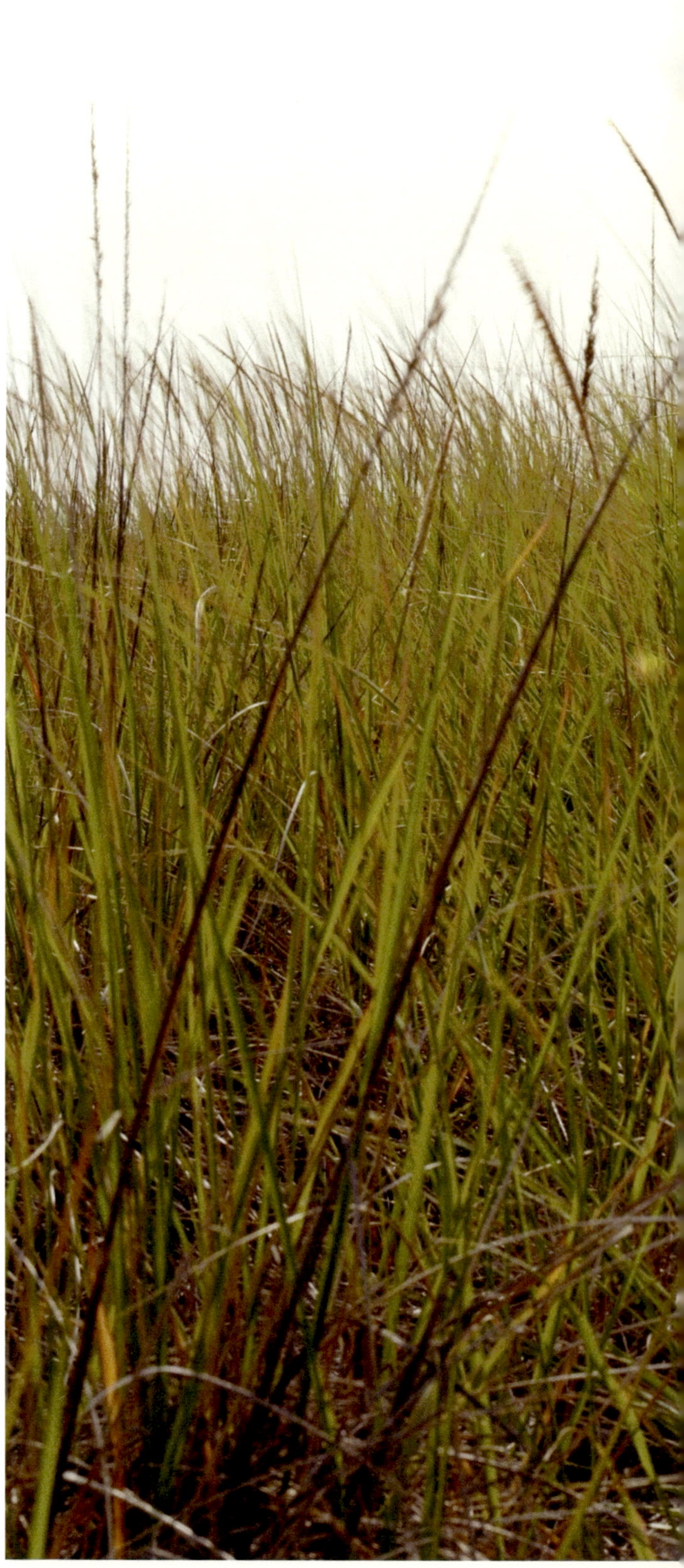

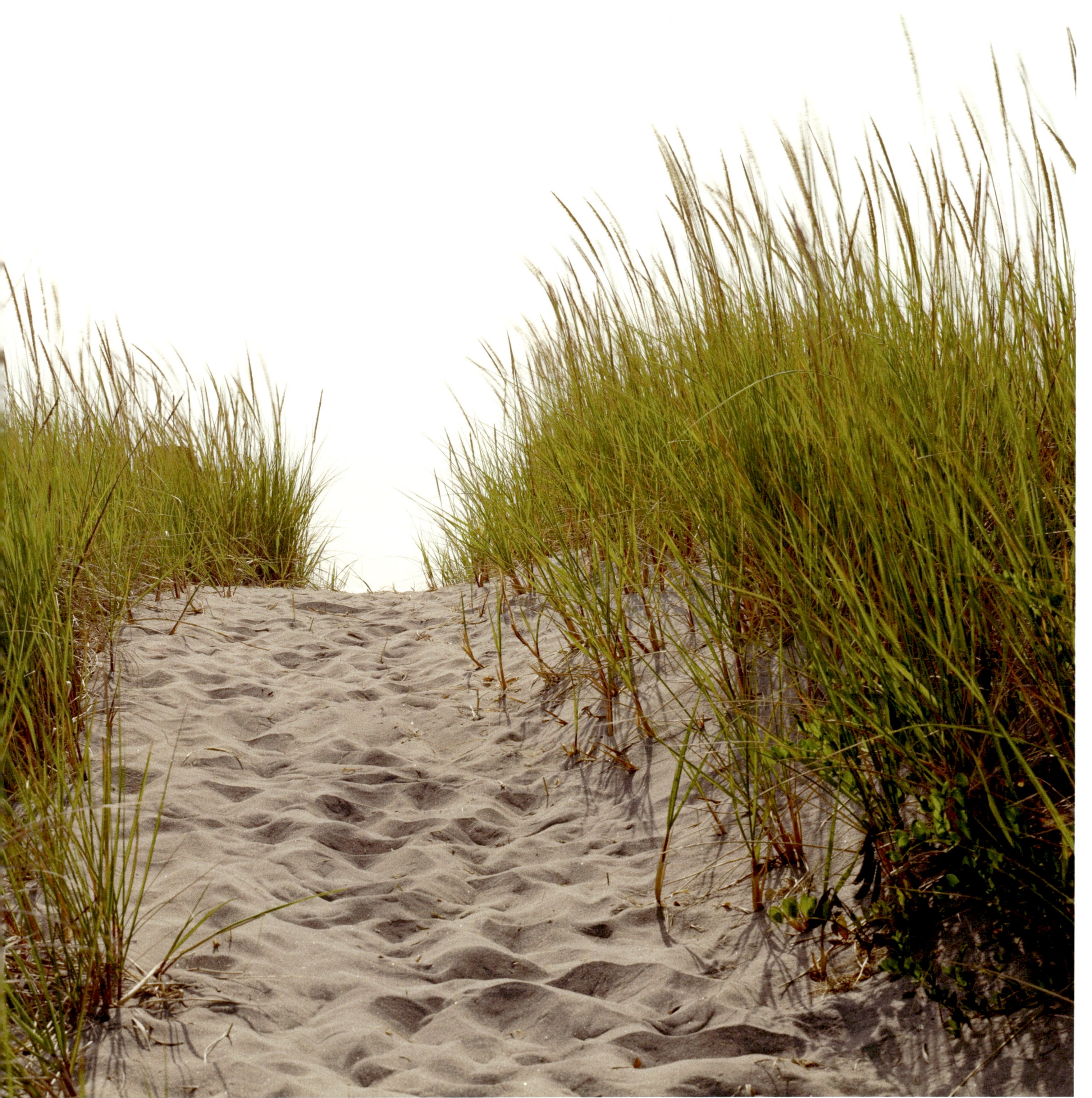

THE WHOLE OCEAN CHANGES
WHEN A STONE IS DROPPED IN IT.

BLAISE PASCAL

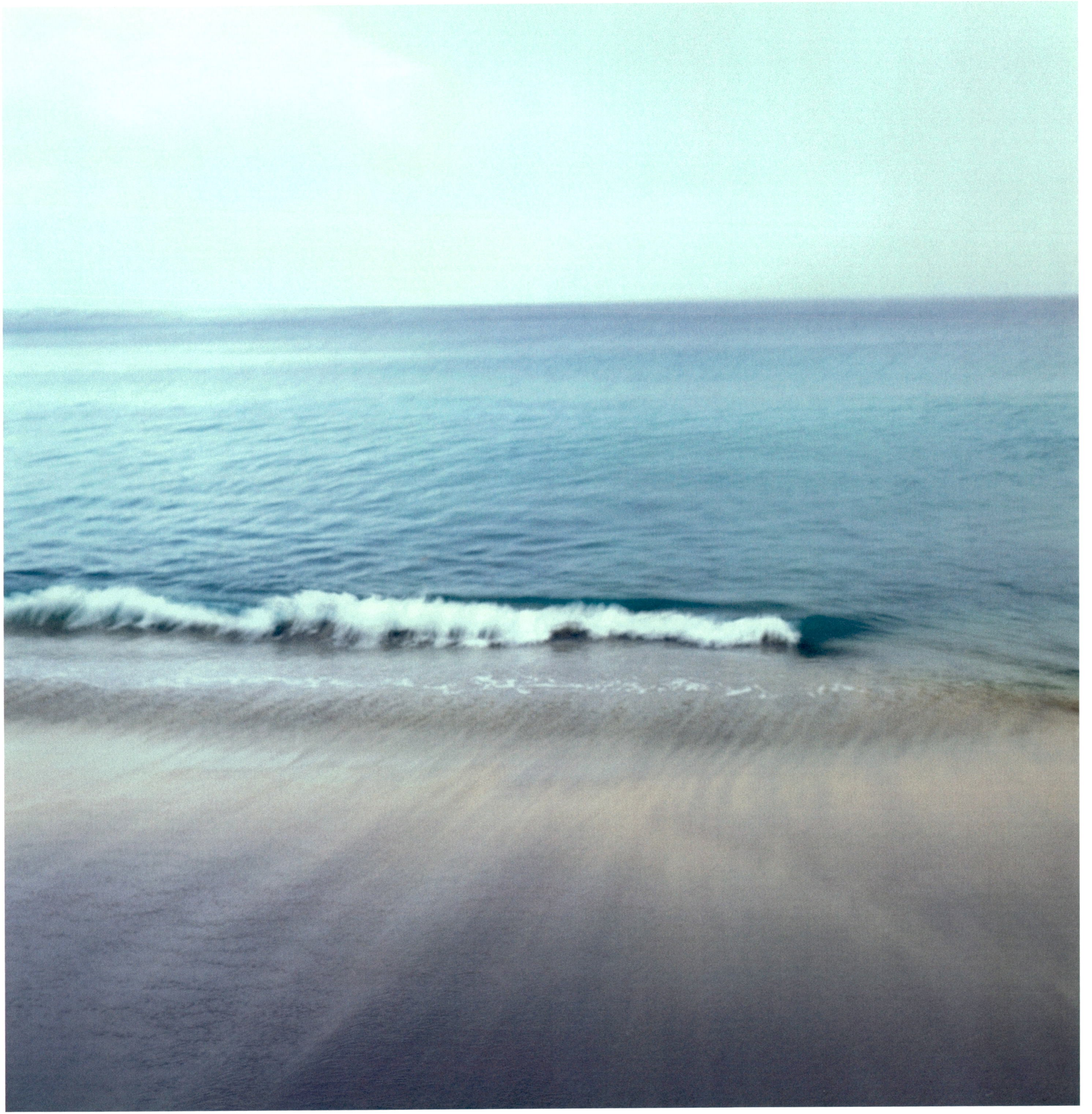

Relaxin'   Moods

CD 01

CD 02

01 **Steven Halpern** – Interstellar Light 4:22
Taken from the album "In the Key of Healing"
Composed by Steven Halpern, published by Open Channel Sound Company

02 **Joel Andrews** – Chakra V: The Throat / Thyroid Chakra 5:09
Taken from the album "Seven Wheels of Light"
Composed by Joel Andrews, published by Sea Gnoms Music, ASCAP

03 **Amit Chatterjee** – Raga Yaman-Kalyan (Excerpt) 5:25
Taken from the album "Colors of the Heart"
Composed by Amit Chatterjee

04 **Dr. Jeffrey Thompson** – Inner Dance 4:10
Taken from the album "Inner Dance", composed by Dr. Jeffrey Thompson

05 **Randy Crafton** – Cross-Talk 5:10
Taken from the album "Inner Rhythms"
Composed and produced by Randy Crafton; recorded and mixed by Jorge Alfano

06 **Jorge Alfano** – Zen Garden 5:45
Taken from the album "Sacred Sounds", composed by Jorge Alfano, BMI;

07 **John Beaulieu** – Harmonic Dance # 1 (Excerpt) 6:06
Taken from the album "Calendula", composed by John Beaulieu

08 **Boris Mourashkin** – Enchantment of the White Lotus 3:30
Taken from the album "Points Of Light"
Produced and composed by Boris Mourashkin

09 **Jim Oliver** – Harmonic Resonance # 2 (Excerpt) 4:10
Taken from the album "Harmonic Resonance"
Composed by Jim Oliver, ASCAP

10 **Laraaji** – Circulation 6:03
Taken from the album "Cascade", composed by Edward Larry Gordon, BMI

11 **Will Seachnasaigh** – Mali (Excerpt) 4:30
Taken from the album "Dreamings"
Composed by Will Seachnasaigh, BMI

12 **Yaya Diallo** – N' Peen (Excerpt) 3:30
Taken from the album "Dombáa Folee"
Composed by Yaya Diallo, produced by Jorge Alfanoy"

01 **Brain Scott Bennett** – Journey 6:00
Taken from the album "Music Meditation: Awaken"
Composed & Produced by Brian Scott Bennett (BMI), Published by Directional Space Music (BMI)

02 **Silvia Nakkach** – Invocation 7:05
Taken from the album "Music Meditation: Unwind"
Produced by Silvia Nakkach and Hans Christian

03 **Amit Chatterjee** – Raga Bhairavi 6:00
Taken from the album "Colors of the Heart"
Amit Chatterjee: Vocals, Sitar and Tanpura

04 **Barry Bernstein M.T.-B.C.** – Move 6:00
Taken from the album "Spirals"
Composed by Barry Bernstein, Randy Crafton, Allaudin Ottinger, Pete Barnhart,
Produced, Recorded and Mixed by Randy Crafton

05 **Ronnie Nyogetsu Seldin** – Echigo-Sanya 5:00
Taken from the album "Komuso"
Recorded at: Sacred Sound Studio, New Jersey, USA

06 **David Darling** – Lady Child's Dream 18:00
Taken from the album "Musical Massage: Balance"
Produced by David Darling, David Darling appears courtesy of: ECM Records, Hearts of Space Recordings,
and Valley Entertainment, All Compositions by David Darling, Tasker/EV-Web Music (ASCAP)

07 **Larraji** – Circulation 5:56
Taken from the album "Cascade"
All Compositions by Edward Larry Gordon BMI, Produced by Jorge Alfano

08 **Dr. Joseph Nagler** – Sapphire 6:31
Taken from the album "Musical Massage: Synergy"
Produced by Dr. Joseph Nagler, All compositions Copyright Dr. Joseph Nagler, ARD NYC Music, ASCAP

09 **César Berlanga** – Prelude and Lullaby for an Old Tree 5:54
Taken from the album "Corazon Espanol"
All compositions by César Berlanga, Produced by César Berlanga

10 **Janetta Petkus** – Kapha 6:00
Taken from the CD "Music for Ayurveda: Kapha"
Produced by Janetta Petkus, Composed by Janetta Petkus

CD 1 & 2: all tracks licensed from "The Relaxation Company", Bayville (USA)
With kind permission of "The Relaxation Company", Bayville (USA) / Q-rious Music (Germany)
This compilation (P) 2003 Q-rious Music

Classical

CD 01

01 **Frédéric Chopin** – Nocturne no.17 in B major op.62/1 6:48
Elfrun Gabriel, (P) 1988*

02 **Felix Mendelssohn Bartholdy** – Concerto for piano and orchestra no.2 op.40, Adagio, Molto sostenuto 7:07
Valentin Gheorghiu, Rundfunk-Sinfonie-Orchester Leipzig, Herbert Kegel, (P) 1973*

03 **Louis Spohr** – Nonet in F major, Adagio 8:30
Berliner Oktett, Richard Waage, flute, Arthur Bauer, oboe, (P) 1984*

04 **Nicolai Rimsky-Korsakov** – Capriccio espagnol op.34, Variazioni 5:18
Dresdner Philharmonie, Jörg-Peter Weigle, (P) 1994**

05 **Wolfgang Amadeus Mozart** – Concerto in C major for Flute, Harp and Orchestra K.299 (297c), Andantino 8:57
Johannes Walter, flute, Jutta Zoff, harp, Staatskapelle Dresden, Otmar Suitner, (P) 1975*

06 **Robert Schumann** – Kinderszenen op.15, Träumerei 3:22
Norman Shetler, (P) 1977*

07 **Wolfgang Amadeus Mozart** – Piano sonata in F major K.332 (300k), Adagio 4:58
Cécile Ousset, (P) 1974*

08 **Ludwig van Beethoven** – String quartet in B flat major op.18/6, Adagio, ma non troppo 7:20
Suske-Quartett, (P) 1977*

09 **Wolfgang Amadeus Mozart** – Piano sonata in B flat major K.333 (315c), Andante cantabile 5:54
Cécile Ousset, (P) 1974*

10 **Franz Danzi** – Wind quintet in G minor op.56/2, Andante 4:16
Ma'alot Quintett, (P) 1993**

11 **Wolfgang Amadeus Mozart** – String quartet no.16 in E flat major K.428 (412b), Andante con moto 7:01
Suske-Quartett*, (P) 1974

* VEB Deutsche Schallplatten Berlin
** edel records GmbH

Moods

CD 02

01 **Wolfgang Amadeus Mozart** – Piano sonata in A major K. 331, Rondo "alla turca" 3:15
Rolf-Dieter Arens, (P) 1990*

02 **Wolfgang Amadeus Mozart** – Piano concerto no.21 in C major K.467, Andante 6:16
Annerose Schmidt, Dresdner Philharmonie, Kurt Masur, (P) 1973*

03 **Franz Schubert** – Moment musical op.94/3 f-Moll 1:37
Dieter Zechlin, (P) 1972*

04 **Frédéric Chopin** – Prelude in D flat major op.28/15, "rain drop" 5:09
Marc Laforet, (P) 1994**

05 **Johannes Brahms** – Piano concerto no.2 in B flat major, Allegretto grazioso 9:19
Cécile Ousset, Gewandhausorchester Leipzig, Kurt Masur, (P) 1976*

06 **Ludwig van Beethoven** – Piano sonata in C Minor op.13 „Pathetique", Rondo. Allegro 4:03
Dieter Zechlin, (P) 1968*

07 **Fréderic Chopin** – Etude in C minor op.10/12 "Revolution" 2:32
Siegfried Stöckigt, (P) 1966*

08 **Maurice Ravel** – Piano concerto in G major, Adagio assai 11:43
Rolf-Dieter Arens, Rundfunk-Sinfonie-Orchester Berlin, Heinz Rögner, (P) 1987*

09 **Felix Mendelssohn Bartholdy** – Song without words op.19/1 3:29
Renate Schorler, (P) 1976*

10 **Wolfgang Amadeus Mozart** – Piano concerto no.25 in C major K.503, Allegretto 9:44
Annerose Schmidt, Dresdner Philharmonie, Kurt Masur, (P) 1973*

11 **Sergej Rachmaninov** – Etude tableaux in F minor op.33/1 2:28
Siegfried Stöckigt, (P) 1966*

12 **George Gershwin** – Rhapsody in Blue 15:53
Siegfried Stöckigt, Gewandhousorchester Leipzig, Kurt Masur, (P) 1977*

* VEB Deutsche Schallplatten Berlin
** edel records GmbH

CD 1 & 2: this compilation (P) 2003 edel CLASSICS GmbH